D1333083

OLD GALLOWAY

UNIFORM WITH THIS BOOK

*

OLD MENDIP
by Robin Atthill

OLD DEVON
by W. G. Hoskins

OLD SOUTHAMPTON SHORES
by J. P. M. Pannell

OLD YORKSHIRE DALES
by Arthur Raistrick

OLD DORSET
by M. B. Weinstock

OLD COTSWOLD
by Edith Brill

OLD NOTTINGHAM
by Malcolm I. Thomis

OLD LIVERPOOL
by Eric Midwinter

OLD LAKELAND
by J. D. Marshall

OLD GALLOWAY

IAN DONNACHIE
and
INNES MACLEOD

DAVID & CHARLES
NEWTON ABBOT   LONDON
NORTH POMFRET (VT)   VANCOUVER

0 7153 6459 6

© Ian Donnachie and Innes Macleod 1974

Set in 11 on 12pt Garamond, and printed in Great
Britain by Latimer Trend & Company Ltd Plymouth
for David & Charles (Holdings) Limited South
Devon House Newton Abbot Devon

Published in the United States of America by David
& Charles Inc North Pomfret Vermont 05053 USA

Published in Canada by Douglas David & Charles
Limited 3645 McKechnie Drive West Vancouver BC

Contents

List of Illustrations

PLATES

List of Illustrations

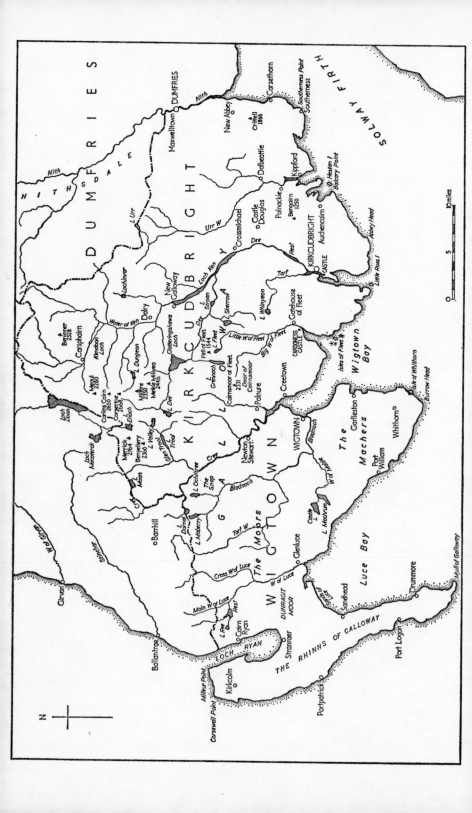

CHAPTER ONE

History and heritage

Galloway is the old traditional name for that beautiful corner of south-west Scotland which now forms the western two-thirds of the new local government region of Dumfries and Galloway. Here a dramatic environment combining mountain, moor, loch and the coastal estuary of the Solway Firth provides the setting for a distinctive history and heritage. This heritage and environment are among the major economic resources of the region, which has a growing tourist and retirement industry. The majority of holidaymakers come to the area to enjoy its peace and quiet and visit its places of historic interest—a whole range of exciting features from prehistoric stone circles and Iron Age hillforts to country villages and Palladian mansions. Galloway also has outstanding artistic associations (which date back to the late nineteenth-century Impressionist years) and when history and art combine the result is remarkable. There must be few parts of Britain where it is possible in a day to see fourth and fifth-century crosses—as at Whithorn and Kirkmadrine—and twentieth-century sculpture by Epstein, Moore and Rodin—on view at the unique moorland art gallery at Shawhead near Castle Douglas.

History has done much to create the distinctiveness of the old province. The twelfth-century Lordship of Galloway was an enormous area stretching from Ettrick Forest in the east to the shores of Carrick in the west. In spite of English incursions during the Wars of Scottish Independence, Galloway survived as a virtually autonomous province till the mid-fifteenth century. By the sixteenth century, Galloway consisted roughly of the shire of Wigtown and the Stewartry of Kirkcudbright—a remote, mysterious region, reaching from the 'brae of Glenapp to the Brig En' o' Dumfries'. Even by the seventeenth century the province was relatively isolated from the rest of the country, still an area of warring clans, religious strife, gipsies, smugglers and coastal raiders. Such an atmosphere provides an essential background to the following three chapters, for although Andrew Symson in his *Large Description of Galloway* provides pointers to a slowly changing economic environment, the survival of fortified houses and contemporary waves of religious persecution and witchcraft indicate a level of social development more typical of the medieval period.

Yet, by the beginning of the eighteenth century, Galloway was in the vanguard of agrarian development; even in the latter half of the previous century there is ample evidence of an expanding and profitable livestock and arable economy, based on the exploitation of native and imported cattle and the export of oats and barley. Admittedly the activities of some landlords undertaking enclosure provoked reaction by displaced tenant farmers and cottars, resulting in a popular protest of dyke-breaking Levellers during the mid-1720s. Later in the century the course of agrarian change quickened, with the majority of local gentry, like William Craik of Arbigland, James Murray of Broughton and Cally, the earls of Galloway and Stair turning their attention to estate 'improvement' and more general economic development. Robert Heron, on his journey through Galloway in 1792, was able to see and describe the changes which had already taken place, including significant industrial and transport developments, the creation of landed estates, the erection of Palladian country houses and planned villages, like those at Gatehouse, Castle Douglas and Garlieston. It is worth remembering that the modern visitor to Galloway looks out on a landscape that is almost entirely the creation of man over the last two hundred years.

Despite the growth of a variety of processing, textile and mining activities during the Industrial Revolution period, agriculture and the land continued to provide throughout the nineteenth century—as they do today—the basis of the regional economy and way of life. The prosperity of farming largely depended on Galloway's long-established sea-borne trade with surrounding industrial districts to north and south, and even when the railway reached most of the area in the 1860s many of the old Solway ports retained their shipping. A new phenomenon created by the railway was the increasing number of tourists and holidaymakers visiting the area, so that by the turn of the century the popularity of Galloway as a holiday centre was well established.

Much of the history described in the case-studies which make up this book has left physical vestiges of outstanding interest. The landscape of Galloway itself is an omnipresent reminder of eighteenth-century agricultural change: field patterns, dykes, ditches, hedgerows, plantations, roads and farm buildings are simple elements in a complex man-made landscape. The short-lived Industrial Revolution in Galloway—largely based on water-power—has left a rich heritage of industrial archaeology, and the planned estate villages and old turnpike roads linking them are evidence of the once close relationship between land and industry. The landscape and its constituent elements are thus clearly primary sources of inestimable value to the historian. The scope for local research based on field study (ranging from prehistoric hill-forts to industrial archaeology) is enormous; the majority of themes in this book place considerable emphasis on field research as well as providing pointers to other possibilities both in Galloway and elsewhere.

More conventional historical source material for Galloway is just as rich and diverse. There are major documentary collections containing regional material in the Scottish Record Office and the National Library of Scotland in Edinburgh, while the Ewart Library and the Museum in Dumfries and Broughton House in Kirkcudbright have smaller catalogued collections. Most of the documentary material consists of family and estate papers, diaries, accounts and business records. There is also an interesting range of local authority records, the majority held either in the Scottish Record Office or by the originators. Early maps and plans of eighteenth or nineteenth-century origin are perhaps the most significant single source for the agricultural and industrial historian, although clearly they are of great value for all kinds of social and economic history. Another important source is provided by old prints and photographs, and Galloway was fortunate to be so well recorded by nineteenth-century artists and photographers. Some of their work illustrates this book. Essential printed source material includes the *Statistical Accounts* and a wide range of Parliamentary Papers, dealing with social and economic conditions. Secondary sources, consisting essentially of regional and local histories, are notable for their bulk and inevitably vary greatly in quality. Again, Galloway was fortunate in its treatment by Victorian antiquaries and historians and there are some excellent local histories.

Historians of the past in Galloway—with a few notable exceptions—have concerned themselves too much with the minutiae of family history; the historiography of the region is thus dominated by a 'gilt on the gingerbread' approach to the past, with the emphasis on clearly identifiable personalities and places. It largely ignores not only ordinary folk in their day-to-day lives, but also the economic and social phenomena of the most dramatic period in the region's history—the agrarian and industrial revolutions of the late-eighteenth and early-nineteenth centuries. Some of the best regional history has appeared in occasional publications and in the pages of the *Transactions of the Dumfries and Galloway Natural History and Antiquarian Society*, a selection from which is provided in the chapter notes at the end of this book.

Here, then, is a series of essays on the history of Galloway since the seventeenth century, with the emphasis on social and economic history and on the remains which can still be seen on the ground —whether the total historic landscape, or minor features within it, such as churches, country water-mills or tower houses. The authors hope that the book will provide an enjoyable introduction to a superb region of Scotland and serve as a useful guide to the possibilities presented by local historical research for professional or amateur historians, and school, college and university students.

References for this chapter are on page 159

CHAPTER TWO

Andrew Symson's Galloway

Andrew Symson's *Large Description of Galloway* was part of a planned geographical survey of Scotland initiated in 1682 by Sir Robert Sibbald, Geographer Royal for Scotland to Charles II. Symson's report was, in effect, a miniature statistical account, especially detailed for the Machers area of Wigtownshire, much more complete than most of the accounts sent in to Sibbald, and immensely useful source material for social and economic conditions in seventeenth-century Galloway. Symson's manuscript version, prepared in Kirkinner in 1684 and revised with additions in 1692, lay among the Sibbald Papers in the Library of the Faculty of Advocates in Edinburgh until 1823 when it was edited by Thomas Maitland, later Lord Dundrennan, and published in Edinburgh. It was subsequently included as an appendix, together with some highly inaccurate biographical data, in William Mackenzie's *History of Galloway* (1841), and more recently in Walter Macfarlane's *Geographical Collections* (Scottish History Society, 1907).

Andrew Symson was born c 1638, probably in England, and educated at the High School of Edinburgh and the University there, graduating MA in 1661. He was licensed to preach by the Bishop of Edinburgh in January 1663 and settled in Kirkinner parish in Wigtownshire during spring that year. A good deal of information about Symson's work in Galloway as rector of Kirkinner 1663–86 is available from the dedication and preface to his *Tripatriarchicon* and from his *Elegies*. Perhaps he does exaggerate his own magnanimity and the general harmony and friendly relationships established with his parishioners:

... my Lot was cast in a very pleasant place ... with a very well natur'd people, who ... payed me great deference and respect ... so that I was for the most part free from those Male-treatments that many of my Brethren mett with ...

It is clear, however, that his parishioners did not attend his church services and that he depended at times upon his friendship with the Earl of Galloway for protection against his neighbours and the 'hill-men'.

Symson was, in fact, at the centre of ecclesiastical affairs in Galloway in his capacity as clerk to the Synod of Galloway from May 1665. The records of the Synod, published by Nicholson in Kirkcudbright in 1856, provide a useful picture of its work—a programme of regular visitation and inspection of parish clergy to examine their qualifications, doctrine, life and conversation; of the persecution of Quakers, Catholics, Covenanting laity and ousted ministers keeping conventicles and secret meetings, and of charmers and necromancers; and of supervision of the usual cases of moral discipline, principally incest and adultery.

In spite of it all, the impression remains that Symson contrived to live a peaceful life and was a more moderate and tolerant man than the Synod's record of heretic hunting and clergy bashing might suggest. Eventually, it was the turn of the Episcopalian clergy and laity to be persecuted and to suffer from the equally ruthless and malignant intolerance of their opponents. Symson, however, had removed to the parish of Douglas in 1686, and from there to Edinburgh to begin a new career as publisher and bookseller sometime between 1689 and 1692. He occupied a tenement in the Cowgate as his printing office, house and book-shop, producing a number of mainly ecclesiastical, devotional and legal publications until his death in January 1712.

Very little is revealed of Symson's family life. Virtually the only information is in the household returns for Kirkinner parish on 15 October 1684, where the occupants of the manse are listed as Andrew Symson, his wife Jane Inglis, his sons Andrew and David, and four others, presumably servants. His third son, Matthias, was not included, probably because he would still have been under twelve years of age.

As an author, Symson may have been over-eager to see himself in print; this is particularly true as regards the work for which he might have preferred to be remembered—his long historical-

Page 17 A typical Galloway landscape near Gatehouse-of-Fleet provides the backcloth for the annual dyking competition, an event which has contributed to a revival in this old craft. The field patterns and plantations seen here date from the eighteenth century

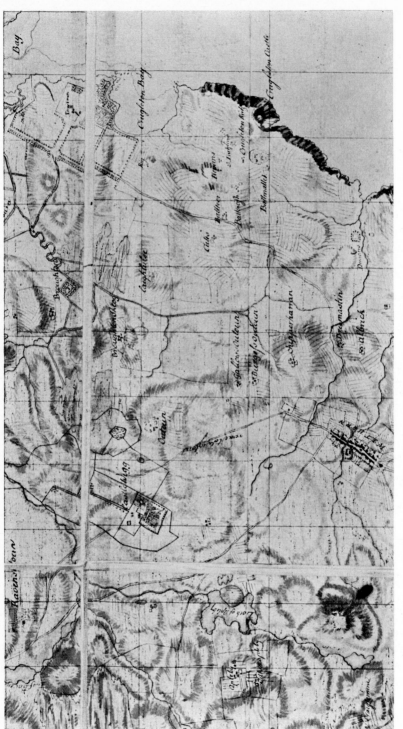

Page 18 Parts of Whithorn, the Castlewigg, Broughton and Cally estates as shown on Roy's map c 1750. Note the formal parks, farm enclosures and roads

anthropological poem, the *Tripatriarchicon*. His obscurity as a poet is well deserved, but Symson in the role of Old Testament scholar is interesting as he tries to relate to Galloway and grapples with the interpretation of a Middle Eastern folk culture with a highly complicated pattern of family relations, in-group and out-group marriage, sacred and profane prostitution, sibling rivalry, incest, concubinage, adultery and polygamy.

There is no doubt that his *Large Description of Galloway* gives an overall impression of reliability, competence, moderation and caution. His personal observation is clearly distinguished from hearsay, practical advice is mixed with the occasional flash of delicate humour, and a proper restraint is observed in descriptions of prehistoric and medieval monuments (for instance, in discussing mottes he says 'when or for what use they were made, I know not'). Sources of possible error are modestly admitted:

> it is hardly possible, after the greatest care and diligence, to be exact, especially where we must of necessitie make use of informations, which we receave from severall hands; and therefore these papers, upon the same account, being liable to mistakes.

He seems to have been a kindly, sensible and detached scholar who really enjoyed working, finding that books were, in his words, 'my delight, my heart, worth nectar and ambrosia in my right hand, believe me a very feast'.

The outstanding value of Symson's *Description* lies in his practical interest in recording farming methods and technology generally. Although he may have been aware of the possibility of change and improvement and might have seen some of the handbooks on animal husbandry circulating in England in the later seventeenth century, he was writing long before the changes which came to south-west Scotland as part of the Agrarian Revolution during and after the second quarter of the eighteenth century (see Chapter Five). If Scotland in 1684 was one of the poorer countries in western Europe, Galloway in turn was seen by travellers as an undeveloped and backward region within Scotland. Even a traveller favourably disposed to the area, John Macky, commenting on the Rhinns of Wigtownshire some years later wrote that, 'I cannot help saying, it's the coursest Part of all the Kingdom, hardly excepting Lochaber and Ross.' Internal disorder and conflict and the absence of effective agencies of central government made progress difficult. Famines were common, as crops were often partial or complete failures. The economy was primarily a primitive, largely self-sufficient, agrarian and static one, with rents paid in kind, often cattle. Internal commerce was conducted principally at fairs and markets (Symson provides a particularly full description of those held at Wigtown), and towns were miserable places with little trade or industry.

Travellers, such as Thomas Tucker in 1655, describe a landscape consisting mainly of moorland or bog, undrained, with no dykes or fences, and with extensive areas of surface water, loch and marsh. There was very little woodland apart from a few patches of old forest, although one or two lairds had begun to establish plantations near their residences. The Provost of Glasgow describes the country from Dumfries to Carlingwark in 1688 as 'a wide expanse of bleak moss, extending for miles on either side, overgrown with whins and broom, and destitute of enclosures of trees, with only a few isolated cottages or a farmhouse to show habitation'. Roads were little more than mud tracks and land journeys often involved long detours to reach the few bridges across the main rivers. Transport methods were still primitive; the creel or 'carr' conveyance was a wicker basket between two shafts, which were tied to a horse and dragged along the ground. Wheeled carts did not come into general use until after the middle of the eighteenth century.

The well-known Pont maps—or rather the versions produced from Pont's manuscript maps by Robert Gordon of Straloch as cartographic editor (1636–48) and published in Johan Blaeu's *Atlas Novus* in Amsterdam (1654)—though variable in accuracy, confirm many of these general points and are useful comparative data. Timothy Pont (c 1560–1630) had surveyed virtually the whole of Scotland between 1584 and 1601, working in Galloway c 1595. On a scale of about 1in to 2·7 miles, the Gordon-Pont maps are a rich source of information on rural settlement patterns, showing towns, churches, water-mills, castles and stockaded tower houses, and other habitations.

The land was divided up between a number of small estates, with tenants in the low country living in self-sufficient farming settlements or 'fermtouns' of six or seven dwellings, each large enough to supply the labour force necessary to look after their cattle, horses, and crops. The 1684 parish lists for Wigtownshire and Minnigaff provide a record of the occupants of some of these settlements. The farms were overstocked with cattle and horses, and there was little or no selective breeding for quality or improvement. Although the development of cattle ranching on a large scale is mainly a post-1707 feature, Symson does mention Sir David Dunbar's exceptional enterprise at his park at Baldoon near Wigtown which

> can keep in it, winter and summer, about a thousand bestiall, part whereof he buys from the countrey, and grazeth there all winter, other part whereof is of his owne breed; for he hath neer two hundred milch kine, which for the most have calves yearly. He buys also in the summer time from the countrey many bestiall, oxen for the most part, which he keeps till August or September; so that yearly he ether sells at home to drovers, or sends to Saint Faiths, Satch, and other faires in England, about eighteen or twentie score of bestiall.

Symson differentiates clearly between the low country people, with an economy based on cattle, barley and long-bearded oats, and the 'moor-men', living in smaller settlements and shielings, herding sheep and growing crops of rye. Minnigaff seems to have been an important meeting place: 'It hath a very considerable market every Saturday, frequented by the moormen of Carrick, Monnygaffe, and other moor places, who buy there great quantities of meal and malt, brought thither out of the parishes of Whitherne, Glaston, Sorbie, Mochrum, Kirkinner, etc . . .'

Standards of farming, the tools and implements used (such as the heavy and clumsy plough drawn by eight or ten oxen), and the system of tillage had probably altered little for centuries. Crops were produced on the in-field and out-field system. Half the land, the in-field adjacent to the farm, was farmed, all of it growing barley each year and one-third of it receiving manure annually. The out-field was divided into four parts, one of which was used as a cattle pound and the rest for grey oats. After being reaped, stooked, stacked in a barn, and threshed with a long, jointed wooden flail, the grain was dried in kilns on a layer of drawn straw or a linen sheet placed over cross-struts near the top of the inside of a 6–7ft-high oval or circular stone structure with a fireplace in the outside wall and a flue into the kiln. Some splendid examples of grain-drying kilns can be seen at Pulmaddy and Carminnow north of Dalry near the A713, in and near Knockman

Wood north of Minnigaff, and at Cruffock beside the Little Water of Fleet north of Gatehouse-of-Fleet (see p 103).

Symson provides a graphic picture of some of the work involved at different stages, the tilling of the oatland and the hulling or 'lomeing' of the oats before milling:

> ... their oatland ... in the Shire, they till not ordinarly with horses, but with oxen; some onely with eight oxen, but usually they have ten ... In severall parts of the Stewartrie, they till with four horses, all abreast, and bound together to a small tree before which a boy, or sometimes a woman leads, going backwards. In the meantime, another stronger man hath a strong stick, about four feet long, with an iron-hook at the lowest end thereof, with which, being put into another iron, fastned to the end of the plough-beame, and leaning upon the upper end of the stick, and guiding it with his hands, he holds the plough-beam up or down, accordingly as he finds the ground deep or shallow ...
>
> The oates, in the Shire, are commonly very bad ... having long beards or awnds ... However, the countrey people have the dexterity of making excellent and very hearty meal ... shelling it in the mill twice, and sometimes thrice, before they grind it into meal ... before they carry the corne to the mill, after it is dry'd in the killn, they lay it upon the killn-flour in a circular bed, about a foot thick; then, being barefoot, they go among it, rubbing it with their feet (this they call lomeing of the corne), and by this meanes the long beards or awnds are separated from the corne, and the corne made, as they terme it, more snod and easie to pass through the mill, when they are shelling of the corne there.

Symson frequently mentions fishing in the rivers and tidal estuaries, describing the taking of salmon with leister, spear and rod and with dogs at the open weekend, on the Dee at Tongland; the fish yards at the mouth of the Luce, and the techniques of fishing with 'halfe-net' in the Bladnoch estuary. Nothing was wasted. Eels taken at the head of the Water of Malzie about Martinmas were salted 'with their skins on, in barrells' and in the winter time eaten 'roasted upon the coals . . . then only pilling off their skins'. The skins were later used for tying and fastening purposes.

The self-sufficiency of the economy is well illustrated by Symson. Oil for lamps was obtained from whales stranded near Wigtown; salt from sea-water in salt-pans in Glenluce and Kirkmaiden; and fuel from bracken, whins and peats; while purple and orange dyes were made from cork-lit and lichens found in Minnigaff, and sacks and ropes from hemp-rigs kept by both moor-men and low-country men adjacent to their dung-hills:

> many of the cords, which they use in harrowing, are made of hemp yarne of their own growing or spinning, which they twine, twentie or thirtie threads together, according to the greatness of the cords they designe to make, and then they twist three ply of this together very hard, which done, they let them ly in bark 'woose', which they say keeps the cords the longer from rotting.

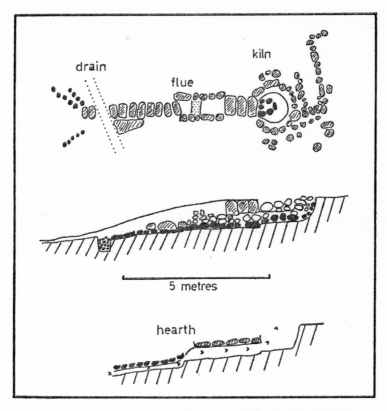

A corn kiln: plan, section and elevation (after J. Scott Elliot). Kilns of this type were a common feature of farmsteads isolated from country meal mills and ruined examples can be found in many parts of Galloway on the sites of abandoned crofts

Mortar for buildings was obtained from shells burned in kilns.

Upon an even area . . . they set erected peits, upon which they put a
layer of shells, a foot thick or more, and then upon them again lay
peits . . . and so, stratum super stratum, till they bring it to an head
like a pyramis; but as they put on these layers just in the center, they
make a tunnel of peits, like a chimney, hollow in the middest, reaching from the bottom to the top . . . this done, they take a pan full of
burning peits and put them down into this tunnel, or chimney, and
so close up all with shells. This fire kindles the whole kilne and in
twentie-four hours space, or thereby, will so burn the shells that they
will run together in an hard masse; after this, they let it cool a little,
and then with an iron spade they bring it down by degrees, and
sprinkling water thereon, with a beater they beat it, or berry it . . .
and then put it so beaten into little heaps, which they press together
with the broad side of their spade, after which, in a short time, it will
dissolve . . . into a small white powder, and it is excellent lime.

Symson also has a superb description of the method used by the
moor-men for tanning cow-hides with a liquid made by steeping
the shoots of heather, instead of bark. The tanned hides were then
used by country shoe-makers.

Perhaps this shows just how primitive a society and an economy
it was. Life was essentially brief, bleak and brutal. The expecta-
tions men had for their lives were minimal. It was much easier to
see life in terms of the passage of the soul through a short disease-
ridden and trialsome existence than to expect to enjoy life for its
own sake. It is quite fundamental to an understanding of the
seventeenth century to realise not only that Symson was writing
for an audience for whom biblical stories and metaphors were still
rich in meaning, but also that he and his readers made quite basic
concepts and assumptions—for example, about the placing of
boundaries between the physical and the spiritual world—which
are alien to twentieth-century readers. It was assumed that the
material environment responded to man's moral behaviour, that
unusual happenings in the natural world were probably portents
of judgements to come. Men were deeply interested in natural
phenomena, such as eclipses, apparitions in the sky, thunder and
lightning, earthquakes in Jamaica, not just as curiosities but because these were regarded as commentaries on and consequences
of other human conditions. The most interesting case that
Symson mentions was from Minnigaff parish:

... not many years since, at a place called La Spraig, not far from the water of Munnach, but sixteen miles distant from the sea, there fell a shower of herring, which were seen by creditable persons who related the story to me. Some of the said herring were, as I am informed, taken to the Earl of Galloway's house and shown to him.

When Symson records remarkable recoveries and instances of individual longevity, this interest should be seen in relation to the general precariousness and shortness of life, and the high incidence of disease and death at this period. Among these recorded cases are those of Margaret Blain, wife to John McCraccan, a tailor in Wigtown, 'brought to bed of three children . . . having a quarter of a year or thereabout before that miscarried of another'; Patrick Makelwian, born in Whithorn in 1546, minister of Lesbury in Northumberland for fifty years, in 1657 in his 110th year, preaching hour-and-a-half-long sermons, having five children after his eightieth year 'four of them lusty lasses, now living with him', his sight becoming clearer, growing new hair on his bald skull, and with two new teeth having appeared in his upper and lower jaw; and Lady Castle Stewart's grandmother, whose sight was restored seven years after she lost it.

Medicine was a mixture of herbal and miraculous cures, using the 'osmunda regalis' or 'filix florida' of 'lane-onion' found in the Caumfoord near the loch of Longcastle for repairing broken bones or strains, and danewort from Wigtown, Anwoth churchyard, and the Cruives of Dervagill in Kirkinner in a concoction of leaves and stalks in sea-water to relieve 'paines in the joynts' or rheumatism. Dumfries burgh records in the 1670s and 1680s include some pharmacists' accounts with details of herbal medicines, including powdered drugs in honey and materials for inhalation, and of their suppliers. A great deal of folk medicine in Galloway is still centred round springs and wells with various supposed curative qualities and properties:

Severall of them the countrey people, according to their fancy, alledge to be usefull against severall deseases, being made use of on such particular days of the quarter, which superstitious custome I cannot allow of; and yet I doubt not but there are severall medecinal wells in this countrey, if they were sought out, and experimented by men capable to judge thereanent.

The Rumbling Well near Buittle was frequented 'by a multitude of sick people, for all sorts of diseases, the first Sunday of May'. The Laird's Croft well near Kilmorie chapel in Kirkcolm and the Muntluck Well near Logan provided predictions on the recovery or death of sick persons. At the latter, which was in the middle of a little bog:

> ... severall persons have recourse to fetch water for such as are sick, asserting (whether it be truth or falsehood, I shall not determine), that, if the sick person shall recover, the water will so buller and mount up, when the messinger dips in his vessel, that he will hardly get out dry shod, by reason of the overflowing of the well; but if the sick person be not to recover, then there will not be any such overflowing in the least.

Local customs listed include the widespread prejudice against cutting down hawthorn trees, and superstitions and omens related to time—for example, washing to cure diseases on the first Sundays of February, May, August, and November in the White Loch of Myrton. Some of these traditions about appropriate and inappropriate times for particular events may have been very old ones:

> Their marriages are commonly celebrated only on Tuesdays or Thursdays. I myself have married neer 450 of the inhabitants of this countrey; all of which, except seven, were married upon a Tuesday or Thursday. And it is look'd upon as a strange thing to see a marriage upon any other days; yea, and for the most part also, their marriages are all celebrated 'crescente luna'.

Such customs doubtless made for communal solidarity, and indeed helped to impose on individuals an identical pattern of life, religion, work and leisure. What is perhaps most remarkable is that men and women had so little freedom to differ in any way from their neighbours without being accused of immorality, heresy or witchcraft. Considering the essential brutality and harshness of their lives, it must have been a relief for ordinary people to escape to the anaesthetising narcotics of whey fermented and barrelled by the moor-men, or ale produced from barley in the low country which had a highly soporific quality from the amount of darnel or 'roseager' it contained; to the chewing of tobacco (to which the country people were much addicted), and to visiting the occasional fair:

> In the kirk-yard of Kirkanders, upon the ninth day of August, there

is a fair kept, called St. Lawrence Fair, where all sorts of merchant-wares are to be sold; but the fair only lasts three or four houres, and then the people, who flock hither in great companies, drink and debauch, and commonly great lewdness is committed here at this fair.

References for this chapter are on page 160

CHAPTER THREE

Tower houses

The motorist who drives through Galloway without even leaving the A75 road cannot fail to be impressed by the number of small castle-like towers passed en route. Many are now ancient monuments in the care of the Department of the Environment, and are preserved as tourist attractions—providing a vital link between the economy of modern Galloway and its late medieval heritage.

Essentially the Galloway towers were small fortified houses, designed and built by unknown local architect craftsmen, and in a line of descent from the timber towers and houses of the mottes and moated homesteads of the twelfth and thirteenth centuries. In most of the earlier towers (c 1450–1580) the emphasis was primarily on the practical necessities of defence, both in determining the site on which the tower was built and in the balance between security and comfort in the building itself. Many of the lesser lairds' houses were sited on crannogs in lochs and swamps even in the later sixteenth century. Cardoness Castle is a good example of a large fifteenth-century tower. Probably only Threave Castle on its river island site was really, with its massive tower, a castle in the sense of being a regional military strongpoint. In later towers and in the adaptation of older buildings after the 1580s there was greater emphasis, as in the Place of Sorbie (see plate on p 36), on providing comfort and on display, with protective devices kept to a minimum. In the more settled conditions after 1690 new ideas predominated, with gardens and parks instead of outer defences and the concept of the country house replacing older traditional forms.

The development of tower house architecture and the history of witchcraft and the Covenanting movement in Galloway can be seen in relation to one central characteristic of life between 1450

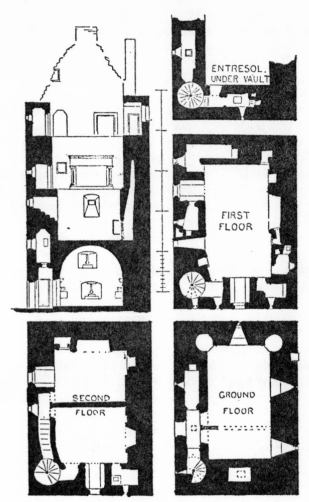

Plans and section of Cardoness Castle

and 1700—the almost constant state of insecurity, political, economic and social, in which people lived. Galloway, economically backward and socially conservative compared to the Scottish Lowlands, shared in the common recurrent disasters of famines, when a bad harvest meant not just rising prices but literal starvation, especially in the terrible year of 1595, and of plagues. Plague regulations in Kirkcudbright in 1578, 1599, 1644

29

and 1648 illustrate the helplessness of public authorities. Only essentially negative reactions were possible—forbidding householders in 1599 to travel beyond the Urr because 'the pest' was in Dumfries, closing the town gates in 1648 to the inhabitants of the neighbouring parishes of Tongland and Kelton, and to beggars and other travellers.

Like other parts of Scotland, Galloway suffered from the anarchy and lawlessness that were inevitable because of the absence of strong central government. The bitter and persistent hostility, virtually a state of perpetual war, between England and Scotland in the fifteenth and sixteenth centuries, and the relative weakness of Scotland, meant that Dumfries-shire, and to a lesser extent eastern Galloway, were subject to almost annual emergencies as English armies raided, looted and burnt castles and towns. Dumfries, for example, was taken by English forces in 1536, 1542, 1547–8, and 1570. Even after 1603, trade barriers between Scotland and England prevented Galloway from taking advantage of its central position in the Scotland–Ireland–Man–north Wales–north-west England area. The records of customs posts between Scotland and England, for example, at Alisonbank on the Sark, are interesting sources for study. Trade in the Solway was further hindered by the activities of pirates, such as Leonard Robertson of Kirkcudbright and his 'men of weir and marrinaris' in the 1570s and Sir Robert Gordon of Lochinvar in the 1620s.

Within Galloway the feuds and quarrels of a brutal, violent, treacherous, and undisciplined nobility, who were the main repositories of territorial power and political influence and who largely controlled the administration of justice through hereditary sheriffdoms and private baronial jurisdictions, made fortified houses a necessity for lords and minor gentry alike. The main families, Maxwells, Gordons, Hannays, Murrays, Stewarts, Kennedys, McCullochs, McKies, McDowalls, MacLellans and others, operated within a kind of 'clan' system, based partly on kinship and partly on bonds whereby weaker lairds followed and served stronger men ('heads of surnames') in return for their protection against raids from neighbours as greedy and possessive as themselves. The development of the Hannay lands through a policy of territorial aggrandisement utilising fortuitous marriage alliances provides one example of the progress of a successful sixteenth-century family. In Galloway generally, young heiresses were married off or kidnapped to obtain possession of their lands; barns were fired, crops stolen, and cattle rustled, and ironically a great deal of time and money was spent in disputes within courts of law—as in medieval society men, whether lairds or townsfolk, were intensely litigious. Neighbours were usually enemies: as were the McDowalls, McKies and Hannays in 1526; the Hannays of Sorbie and Murrays of Broughton in the 1590s and 1600s, in a series of feuds involving the Kennedys, Dunbars and Stewarts of Garlies; and the McCullochs and Gordons as late as the 1660s and 1690s. And sometimes family feuds became confused with quarrels between Catholics and Protestants in the sixteenth century and between Catholics, Episcopalians and Covenanters in the seventeenth century.

One fundamental reason for this persistent quarrelsomeness and violence was probably the shortage of land and lack of opportunities for the younger sons of the lairds. However, the colonial-imperial policies of James VI and I, in particular the Protestant Plantation of Ulster after 1607, helped to provide a source of new lands for members of some Galloway families and to divert their energies into a pseudo-religious crusade to 'root out superstition, plant religion, and civilise the Irish'. It is interesting also, although the affair was not of great practical importance, that a number of Gallovidians, including Sir Robert Hannay of Mochrum, Sir James Stewart of Corsewall, and Sir Robert Gordon of Lochinvar, purchased Nova Scotian baronetcies sold in Scotland in 1625–37. Gordon, indeed, had published a volume of plans for the 'Plantation of Cape Breton, now New Galloway, in America' (1620) which, even if the plan was never implemented, is perhaps a good example of the restless ambitions of men seeking new lands to conquer. In fact conditions in Galloway did improve in the later sixteenth and early seventeenth centuries, but the religious wars and disorders running from the 1630s to the 1680s meant another period of confusion and uncertainty.

Towns had only a relatively inconspicuous place in the economy of Galloway. Thomas Tucker in 1655 and Daniel Defoe on his 1706 visit provide descriptions of undeveloped communities in decay. Although some of the burghs owned large areas of the surrounding countryside—as shown in burgh court minute books, assessment books and town council minute books—Kirkcudbright, Wigtown, Whithorn, Innermessan and Stranraer were too small to be independent of neighbouring lairds who often maintained tower houses within the burgh boundaries: the MacLellans in Kirkcudbright, the Hannays and McCullochs in Wigtown, and the Neilsons, Agnews and McDowalls in Innermessan. The published volumes of Kirkcudbright Town Council records (1576–1658) and Kirkcudbright Sheriff Court Deeds (1623–1700) and the unpublished protocol books of James Glover (1588–1618) and William Gairdner (1595–1615), notaries in Stranraer, provide a detailed picture of the geography of Kirkcudbright and Innermessan and the occupations of the townsfolk.

The jealousies and rivalries between towns, each claiming a narrow monopoly of trade and commerce within its own area, sometimes developed into serious conflict. There were frequent actions within Kirkcudbright Burgh Court against inhabitants of Minnigaff attempting to avoid dues payable to Kirkcudbright; Kirkcudbright opposed the erection of the town of New Galloway by the Gordons of Lochinvar and Earlston in 1629; and Kirkcudbright and Dumfries often clashed over merchants escaping dues payable to Dumfries by unloading cargoes at Carsethorn and in creeks on the Urr. Disputes between the latter reached a head in the 1598 raid on Kirkcudbright by the baillies and burgesses of Dumfries. This expedition to surprise and sack Kirkcudbright was driven off by the townspeople, and eventually Dumfries had to pay damages for destroying barns, probably at Millburn.

Sixteenth- and seventeenth-century burgh records for Dumfries and Kirkcudbright provide ample evidence of expenditure on their defences: enclosures behind private houses and yards held with 'watch and ward' duty to defend the town walls; ditches and earthen banks cut and maintained between the ports, and the ports or gates themselves permanently guarded and barred at night. Both towns were built inside a complex of natural river and swamp barriers. The Kirkcudbright defences were probably the more impressive; the 10–11ft-high walls enabled the town to be successfully defended against an assault by Sir Thomas Carleton's detachment from the English army in February 1547. At the end of this period the reaction of Dumfries to the Jacobite rebellion in 1715 is especially interesting. As in any medieval town, in an emergency the defences were strengthened, entrenchments including halfmoons and bastions dug, the ports refortified with redoubts to cover the entries, and the inhabitants organised in companies to man the barricades and trenches. Some of the men were armed only with 'sythes . . . fixed . . . sufficiently on shafts'.

Throughout much of this period an element of fortification, whether by townsfolk or by country lairds, was necessary to ensure survival. Galloway was divided into a number of small estates each with its power centre in a complex of buildings round a tower variously referred to as a place and fortalice, a tower and manor place, or as a castle ('the Place of the Chapell', 'the tower and manor place of Killaser', 'the castle of Inche'). At least 150 tower houses were built in Galloway during this time. Many survive—in most cases only the site or a stump of the tower remains; others were incorporated in eighteenth- or nineteenth-century houses, such as Kirkconnel, Kenmure Castle, Cassencary, Machermore, Craichlaw, Castlewigg and Ardwell. The Pont-Gordon maps with their stereotyped symbols for castles and towers are a convenient source for the geography of Galloway c 1595 (the original Pont manuscript maps had miniature sketches of each building). Symson's lists of the principal edifices in each parish are useful for Wigtownshire and Minnigaff, and Sir James Balfour's and Sir Robert Sibbald's lists for Galloway as a whole. A great deal of work remains to be done as regards the detailed examination of sites, in order to establish the layout of the complexes of ancillary buildings in relation to the towers and the outer defences, and also as regards excavation, including initially their rubbish heaps.

It was for a time theoretically incumbent upon the holders of land of a certain extent in the Borders to erect towers under a 1535 law as part of a programme of national defence:

> It is statute and ordained for saving of men their goods and gear upon the borders in time of war and of other troublous time, that every landed man dwelling in the inland or upon the borders having there a hundred pound land of new extent shall build a sufficient barmkin upon his heritage and lands in place most convenient of stone and lime . . . for the resset and defence of him his tenants and their goods in troublous times; with a tower in the same for himself if he thinks it expedient. And that all other landed men of smaller rent and revenue build peels and great strengths as they please for saving of themselves, men tenants and goods . . .

Again in theory some control was exercised by the Scottish kings over the building of towers by the issue of licences to crenellate, ie to build a structure with corbelled battlements. Very few licences survive. A good example, concerning a tower house built within a Galloway burgh, is the one issued to Wm Ahannay in 1549:

> Ane letter maid to William Ahannay, burges of Wigtoun and his airis gevand thame full power and fredome to rais and sett furth the heid of his hous, lyand within the burgh on the north side of the Hie Gaitt thairof fornentis the Mercate Croce of the samyn, etc, with battaling and corbell sailze in the maist honest and substantious maner he pleisis and sall think maist expedient . . .

The Galloway laird was a farmer as much as a landowner and his tower was only part of a complex of farm buildings, barns, stables and retainers' quarters built inside a courtyard area, with a stone barmkin wall and perhaps an outer ditched enclosure for the protection of his cattle and horses. The best remaining examples are Garlies Castle, where the inner and outer yards and outbuildings are clearly marked, and Hillis Tower. The important point to remember is that the centrepiece of the whole complex, the tower house, was not necessarily or even usually a freestanding building (as the towers are mostly seen today).

Apart from Threave and the unique little tower at Orchardton, there are few tower houses in Galloway which compare in architectural importance with the elaborate and sophisticated extravaganzas of north-east Scotland, but Cardoness, Carsluith, Rusco, Barholm, Drumcoltran, Hillis, Craigcaffie, Barscobe, Sorbie and Park are good examples of moderately sized Scottish tower houses. The towers were usually of random rubble stonework with perhaps originally rough cast or 'harling'. The earlier towers were usually rectangular, three or four storeys high, each floor often consisting of a single room, with sometimes, as at Carsluith, the later addition of a four- or five-storey wing. Sixteenth-century towers were more often built on the L plan. Doorways in early towers were often at first-floor level with access by ladder or external stair; in later towers the doors were on the ground-floor level and in L-plan towers in the re-entrant angle. Doors and windows were usually protected by iron grating 'yetts' and 'grilles'. The walls were hollowed out into a labyrinth of passages and mural chambers, with a wheel stair either in the wall thickness

Page 35   Threave Castle, showing island site, barmkin wall and tower house

Page 36   The Old Place of Sorbie

Orchardton Tower, from a nineteenth-century engraving

in a corner or in the smaller wing in L-plan towers, and sometimes a separate attic-stair turret.

Defence may have been conducted at first from the top of the tower with projecting timber war-heads or stone corbelling with machicolation, but after c 1480–1500 it was conducted from the ground floor, using small inverted keyhole or dumb-bell gunports for hand guns. In fact, crenellated battlements, pepper-pot corner turrets, cape-houses as lookout points, and machicolation were retained in the sixteenth and seventeenth centuries to appropriately display the status of the occupants. To some extent also gunports were fashionable rather than utilitarian devices. Examples of Renaissance influences are rare, although the gateway at Baldoon is a fine and beautiful piece of work. Outside Galloway proper the Nithsdale range (1638) at Caerlaverock and the oriel windows at Maybole are interesting. On the other hand local craftsmanship and skill can be seen in the fine fireplaces and aumbries at Cardoness, Orchardton, Garlies and Castle Stewart, the richly decorated doorways at Barholm and MacLellan's Castle, and inscriptions with data about the proprietors and panels with heraldic devices above the doors of several towers.

The advice in Latin in the panel above the door at Drumcoltran is very striking:

> Keep hidden what is secret; speak little; be truthful;
> avoid wine; remember death; be pitiful.

Data on life inside these towers is scarce, although household inventories, burgh court records of claims, and auctions of property from the late sixteenth century onwards contain lists of goods and plenishings: dairy, spinning, and weaving equipment; chairs, chests, beds, tapestries, candlesticks, fire-irons; weapons, such as lances, spears, bows, arrows and swords; male dress, including bonnets and swordbelts, breeches, slashed trunk hose and jackets with slashed sleeves, shoes and gloves; and musical instruments, including lute, guitar, tympanis or cymbals, horn, bussonis or bassoon, and harpsichord.

Information about the lives and characters of the men and women who used these things is very meagre. Samuel Rutherford's letters contain the sort of biographical and personal material that is generally lacking. In terms of visual representations the little, probably sixteenth-century, stone in an outhouse at the Meikleyett Nurseries near Kirkcudbright and the head portraits of Sir Thomas MacLellan and his wife Grisel Maxwell on their elaborate monument in Greyfriars church, Kirkcudbright, are interesting. Some men certainly had pretensions to a courtly elegance which must have been rather out of place in Galloway. The courtier and diplomat Patrick Hannay, perhaps the brother of John Hannay of Sorbie and Sir Robert Hannay of Mochrum, was the author of a number of pleasant polished pieces, including 'A Happy Husband or Directions to a Maid to chose her Mate' (1619) and 'A Wifes behavior before marriage' (1619):

> The maple, with a scarry skin,
> Did spread broad pallid leaves:
> The quaking aspen, light and thin,
> To the air free passage gives—
> Resembling still
> The trembling ill
> Of tongues of womankind;
> Which never rest,
> But still are prest
> To wave with every wind.

Tower houses

At the other end of the social scale, it is very difficult to imagine or understand the lives and problems of the mass of ordinary country people living in their chimneyless cottages with sod roofs and central hearths. There was a small merchant class in between and some examples of their domestic architecture survive in the High Street of Kirkcudbright (the Tolbooth Gallery, Ironstanes and 74 High Street). The Kirkcudbright Tolbooth or town house nearby probably started as a defensible tower about 1579 or earlier, with alterations and additions in 1591, 1625, and 1791. The small, later seventeenth-century, two-storey-and-attic house in New Abbey (962662) is another good example of domestic architecture, in this case built by the Stewarts of Shambellie.

References for this chapter are on page 160

CHAPTER FOUR

Witches and Covenanters

It is perhaps not too difficult an historical exercise to imagine
the physical conditions in which men lived in seventeenth-
century Galloway, with plagues, shortness and precariousness
of human life, vulnerability to pain and disease, and general insecurity. It is much more difficult to understand the way people
thought about disasters, to see the logic behind violent fanaticism
and religious frenzy, with men and women (labelled as Covenanters, Episcopalians, witches and charmers) being hunted down
and killed, or to see why political quarrels were defined as religious
crusades. Life in the here and in the hereafter was still seen in
terms of assumptions difficult to recognise from modern liberally
minded agnostic Britain. The creation, the fall of man, the second
coming of Christ and the imminent end of the world were seen
not as metaphorical expressions of truth but as dateable historical
events. The world was a battleground between God and the
Devil, or Anti-Christ, with God and his angels on the one hand
regularly intervening in world affairs and on the other Satan,
trying to steal the souls of men, recognised variously as the Pope,
bishops, the Episcopal Church, Presbyterians, the monarch, false
churches and sects of all kinds. Satan's allies and agents were
working everywhere—witches and enchanters sharing his power
to use curses and spells, demon spirits, heretics, lunatics, persons
driven mad by pain and disease. Rival versions of Christianity
were not just errors, but the worship of Satan.

Galloway was a hotbed of competing superstitions, fears and
hatreds in which, although the strongest hysteria was undoubtedly
anti-Popery, the struggles, martyrdoms and assassinations were
essentially of Protestants by other varieties of Protestants. Religion
did not mean love, charity, tenderness, tolerance or benevolence,
but the imposition of certainties of righteousness by doctrinaire

intellectuals and busybodies. Fanaticism was not the prerogative of one religious group, but rather a phenomenon common to all, Episcopalians and Presbyterians alike, with each group in power using state authorities and local civil courts to impose their brands of orthodoxy, by force if necessary, and prepared to kill and to die for Christ (the classic example being the 1642 Scottish crusade, the Solemn League and Covenant, to attempt to force Presbyterianism on England). The totalitarian authoritarianisms of Episcopalians (1660–89) and Presbyterians (1638–60 and post 1690) were not essentially different, although Presbyterianism was worse in Galloway in the sense of being genuinely popular and therefore more effective in imposing its tyranny. Very full documentation of the beliefs, customs and discipline procedures involved is provided in the seventeenth- and early-eighteenth-century church session minute books and in burgh records.

The Presbyterian church in power was an immensely powerful organisation, the only education authority and social welfare agency, a court of morality interfering, censoring and controlling the most trivial aspects of human behaviour, and extending its multiple intolerances not just to religious opponents, Catholics, Episcopalians, and Quakers, but to nonconforming persons of any variety—outcasts, gipsies, troublemakers. The most obvious discipline imposed was uniformity of worship, including compulsory attendance at Sunday services with elders searching houses and reporting absentees, visiting ale-houses to chase up stragglers, and requiring travellers to produce testimonials to establish how they had spent their Sabbath rests. Informers and agents were employed to pry and provide information; for example, Kirkcudbright burgh in 1639 introduced new rules on Sabbath observance 'for trying quherof thair are secreit spyes appoynted'. Session members, elders and clergy, combined the functions of censors, marriage guidance counsellors and guardians of morality, spending an enormous amount of time examining reports of erotic episodes and sexual irregularities. One real problem here was that Presbyterians and Episcopalians respectively refused to recognise the validity of marriages (or baptisms) by their opposite numbers.

The techniques of torture utilised, punishments imposed and public repentances required were part of the formal apparatus of ecclesiastical and civil policy. That the discipline imposed by Presbyterian sessions and Episcopalian synods or by town councils and courts was savage is not surprising and perhaps reflects a general insensibility to violence in what was, after all, the age of slavery and indentured servitude in the British plantations in the West Indies and America. The heads of executed Covenanters were displayed on the gates of Kirkcudbright and Dumfries; men were burnt to death in Dumfries in 1639 and 1665 for bestiality offences (*Leviticus*, XX, 14–15); thieves in Dumfries and Kirkcudbright were sentenced to be branded on hand, shoulder, or cheek, flogged ('scourgit') throughout the streets, and banished from the town; offenders were publicly humiliated at church door and before the pulpit or in jougs and stocks at the mercat cross; confessions were obtained from witches by the clergy as professional experts and by their agents by means of torture, using racks, pulleys, thumbscrews ('pilliwinkies'), pincers, deprivation of sleep, and examination by 'prodding' using a 3in pin to find the 'unnatural' mark where the Devil had touched the witch's body.

The treatment of cases involving supernatural happenings, sorcery and witchcraft illustrates the interaction between the fantasies of the theologians and the problems and collective fears of ordinary country people. Surviving synod, presbytery, and church session minutes; town council, justiciary court and Privy Council records, and occasional contemporary pamphlets and literacy accounts contain many reports and casual references, although these probably represent only a small proportion of the actual cases in Galloway. Two reports of supernatural happenings recorded in pamphlet literature are classic examples: the case of the Devil of Luce, a spirit which molested the house of a weaver Gilbert Campbell in 1655–6, for which blame was placed eventually on Alex Agnew, a beggar later hanged at Dumfries for blasphemy, who had threatened hurt to Campbell's family because they had not given him alms he needed; and the more famous case of the stone-throwing, minister-attacking spirit which invaded the house of Andrew Mackie, at Ringcroft in Rerrick parish, in 1695 (see plate on p 53), and for which an explanation was perhaps found in the actions of the previous occupant of the house who had sent his son to a sorceress at Routingbridge in Irongray parish to find out the reason for the decay of his person and his goods.

The Luce and Ringcroft cases illustrate the serious consideration which Episcopalian and Presbyterian committees of investigating clergy gave to the activities of spirits and brownies. Even more attention was paid to the works of practitioners of non-ecclesiastical white magic, the charmers and necromancers—'these pillars of the kingdome of darknesse' as minuted by Symson in the Register of the Synod of Galloway—helping and comforting the people by providing protection for the sick and diseased and for cattle, crops and houses. There are numerous references in synod and session records to the examination and punishment of men and women going to charmers, often outside Galloway in Dumfries-shire or in Ayrshire or at least outside their own parishes, or for using simple magic themselves—turning the riddle, metting the belt, turning the key in the Bible, winnowing straw, burning bedstraw, and visiting and making offerings at holy wells. Families of lairds were sometimes involved in these cases, and Galloway nobility were among the patrons of London-based astrologers, such as William Lilly (1602–81), who were consulted by correspondence for advice on finding lost property, propitious sailing dates and personal matters—but, of course, astrology was respectable, still an essential part of courses in medicine and botany. The local Galloway charmers—who combined the roles of psychiatric social workers, veterinary advisers, fortune-tellers and faith healers—played a positive part in Galloway life, providing ritual spells and herbal cures for the ailing, love charms and aphrodisiacs, advice on choosing husbands and wives, and simple divining techniques for finding lost or stolen goods or stock. Another reason for their success was that they provided practical guidance and defence measures—counter-magic—for potential victims of the black magic of witches, brownies and spirits. Such advice included taking three tufts of thatch from above the door of the witch Elspeth Thompson at Screel near Dalbeattie to neutralise her powers, or placing stones with circular holes on the lintels of cow houses to protect the milk yield of the cows.

That may seem a dull type of witchcraft, but it must be said that on the whole in Galloway witchcraft cases related directly to simple, practical agricultural activities and country life. Witchcraft was a heresy involving an alliance with and adherence to the Devil, a concept firmly based on Old Testament studies (*Exodus*, XXII, 18, 'Thou shalt not suffer a witch to live'), but the more truly fantastical elements found in the Scottish Lowlands—covens, cases of sexual assault by incubus, and the activities of familiar imps, usually small animals such as rats, toads, dogs and cats—seem to be either absent altogether or comparative rarities in Galloway. Witchcraft prosecutions under the Scottish Parliament statute of 1563, or under General Assembly Acts of 1640, 1643, 1644, 1645 and 1649, were usually initiated at a local neighbourhood level and examinations conducted before the church sessions where most confessions were obtained, and referred ultimately to the Privy Council who commissioned special judges to hear cases in Ayr, Dumfries, and Kirkcudbright. Sentences were variable, but were usually death by strangulation at the stake with the bodies being subsequently burned ('worried at ane stake till they be dead and theirafter their bodies to be burnt to ashes'), although in cases of extreme wickedness witches were burnt alive. The most spectacular cases must have been the five Wigtownshire women—Marion Shenan in Drochdool, Jonnet McKennan in Balmurrie, Africk Elam in Knockibae, Marion Russell in Glenluce, and Isobell Bigham in Stranraer—tried as witches in 1644, and the nine women—Agnes Comenes, Janet McGowane, Jean Tomson, Margt Clark, Janet McKendrig, Agnes Clerk, Janet Corsane, Helen Moorhead and Janet Callan—strangled and burnt at the Whitesands in Dumfries on 13 April 1659. In cases after 1700 the usual sentence imposed by the kirk sessions was banishment: for example, Jean McMurrie in Irelandton, before Twynholm kirk session in 1703, charged with making milk useless, women ill, and causing the deaths of horses on her neighbours' farms, was banished from the Stewartry; and Janet McRobert of Milnburn, before Kirkcudbright kirk session in 1701, charged with making cows ill, dogs mad, and with having the Devil appear in her house, was banished to Ireland.

Although in seventeenth-century Scotland as a whole there were clearly periods with unusually high incidences of witchcraft prosecutions, particularly 1640–4 and 1690–3, cases in Galloway do not fit into any simple pattern. It is not possible to show, except in very general terms, that they coincided with periods of extreme economic and social pressure, nor it is possible to be certain of the regional distribution of cases within Galloway, although more have been identified in the Stewarty than in Wigtownshire, and few of the witches seem to have been townspeople.

The cases against the witches depended usually upon a series of stereotyped accusations by their neighbours expressing the hostility of a community to someone suspected of causing the disasters which befell them—the failure of their crops, accidents or disease crippling or killing their cows, horses and hens, family illnesses and deaths, all phenomena related to the insecurity of a subsistence economy. The case of Elspeth McEwen from Bogha, near Cubbox in Balmaclellan parish, is a good late example. She was accused of making her neighbours' hens stop laying and of having a movable wooden pin at her command that could draw off milk from their cows. Examined before Dalry kirk session in 1696, she was imprisoned and tortured in Kirkcudbright Tolbooth until she confessed, tried before a commission appointed by the Privy Council, found guilty 'of a compact and correspondence with the devil, and of charms and of accession to malefices', and executed in 1698. The witches themselves seem to have been the most vulnerable and weakest persons in each community, widows or single women, probably old and physically unattractive, and possibly mentally unbalanced, begging for alms and assistance, and threatening and cursing when these were refused, victims of poverty and despair and a harsh and cruel environment—much more innocent victims and more viciously tortured and killed than the young, arrogant, aggressive and fanatical Covenanting 'martyrs'.

A great deal has been written about the Covenanters in Galloway. 'Covenanters' generally meant in this context not the Presbyterians in power, before 1660 and after 1690, but the fanatical group of 'conventiclers', the element amongst the Presbyterians who refused to reconcile themselves to the restoration of Episcopalian church government (1660–89). Their opposition, all the more dangerous because it was a genuinely popular grassroots movement, took the form not only of supporting ousted Presbyterian ministers and holding meetings or conventicles, but also of opposing with sporadic guerrilla warfare, ambushes and assassinations the Episcopalian policy of repression through fines, billeting, executions and banishment to indentured servitude in Jamaica, Barbados and Virginia. The escalation of violence by both Episcopalians and Covenanters reached a peak in the 'killing times', 1685–8.

The really interesting and unanswered questions concern the strength of this hostility to the restoration of Episcopacy in Ayrshire, Galloway and Dumfries-shire. Did it relate in some way to

the English occupations of 1547-9 and the early introduction of
Calvinist ideas and traditions? To what extent can it be explained
in terms of sectional interest and social forces, and how important
was the political opposition of the lairds who controlled the
Presbyterian church to the extension of central government control, taxation, the ecclesiastical and civil authority of the Crown
associated with Episcopacy? Was it an expression of Scottish
nationalism or of regional separatism? A decisive element may
have been aristocratic leadership by local lairds, like the Gordons,
the MacLellans and the Stewarts, and the Earls of Cassilis and
Glencairn. To what degree, for example, were the tenants of
Glenrazie, Corsbie, Barnkirk and Baltersan on Castle Stewart
estate following their superior? Why were the Covenanters
strongest in the hill and moorland parishes—Penninghame in the
northern Machers, Minnigaff, Anwoth and Girthon in the western
Stewartry, and Dalry, Kells, Carsphairn, and Balmaclellan in the
northern Stewartry? Was it then in any way a creed of a depressed
peasantry relating to the economic and social problems of the
hillmen? Were elements of radical politics involved at all com-
parable with the programmes of the Diggers and Ranters in the
upland areas of northern and western England? Many Covenanters were very young men and women, so was it to a degree a
teenage phenomenon?

The importance of the 'conventiclers' was much exaggerated by
eighteenth- and nineteenth-century writers, who were not interested in these sort of questions about them, who forgot that their
heirs were not to be found in the established Presbyterian Church
of Scotland but in groups like the Cameronians and the Macmil-
lanites remaining outside it, and who imagined that their struggles
had something to do with the development of religious liberty and
tolerance in the eighteenth century. In fact, tolerance was really an
eighteenth-century invention, a triumph of expediency over the
religious principles of Covenanters, Presbyterians, and Episcopalians alike, and part of a much wider retreat from the supernatural to the material world. The decline of religious mania in
Galloway was related to other factors: the greater security and the
control of the environment which came with improvements in
technology, agriculture, and seamanship. What an enormous
contrast there is with the Galloway of a hundred years before in
the light-hearted comments of Robert Heron in 1793:

Witches and Covenanters

. . . devils, brownies, witches, fairies are becoming every year, less numerous, and less frequent in their appearance, in Kirkcudbright-shire. It is possible, that they may, in time, share the same fate of the ancient wild cattle which have been entirely exterminated out of this country . . .

References for this chapter are on page 160

CHAPTER FIVE

The Agrarian Revolution and the Levellers

The main source of Galloway's wealth in the past, as at present, was the land. Yet today's landscape differs dramatically from that described by Andrew Symson in the late seventeenth century (see Chapter Two). The modern landscape is largely the creation of the past 300 years, a landscape moulded and created by man and bearing everywhere the imprint of human activity. The elements of this imprint are to be found in the way the land is parcelled into estates and farms; in the regular and irregular fields divided from each other by dry stone dykes; in woodland plantations and shelter belts; and in the roads and tracks which link together settlements ranging from the isolated upland farmstead to the planned, estate village. The transformation largely took place in the eighteenth century, although it had its roots much earlier. The Agrarian Revolution had a major effect on the landscape of Galloway and indeed the Province was one of the first areas of Scotland to be affected by the rise of large-scale, commercial farming, largely for the English markets across the Solway. For the 'improvers'—the men of vision like Sir David Dunbar of Baldoon or William Craik of Arbigland—who initiated changes on their lands, the rewards came in increased profits and rents. The traditional agriculture and the way of life associated with it may not have been upset to quite the extent as were the Highland clan system and crofting by the Clearances, but there were unquestionably many casualties of the change from the old farming system to the new. The reaction against change in the countryside of Galloway, which preceded the creation of sheepruns in the Highlands by as much as a century, was so dramatic, however, that it assumes the aspect of a popular movement. Not until the Crofters' War of the 1880s did rural protest find an outlet quite so organised as that of the Levellers of Galloway—the groups of lesser and tenant farmers who roamed the countryside breaking the dykes of enclosed parks and fields where cattle for the southern markets grazed. Despite initially achieving a measure of success and even winning support for their cause from a few more radical lairds and merchant burgesses, the Levellers were, within a few years of the outbreak of reaction in 1724, reduced to nothing in the face of unstoppable agrarian change.

A brief examination of the old system of agriculture in pre-eighteenth-century Galloway engenders some appreciation of exactly what the Levellers were seeking to defend and an insight into the inevitability of their demise as a rural popular movement. A number of valuable contemporary sources can be called upon, principally Andrew Symson's *Large Description of Galloway*, General William Roy's *Military Survey Map of Scotland*—an invaluable cartographic tool for the historian of landscape in Scotland because it dates from the mid-eighteenth century when much of the change described here was already underway—and Sir John Sinclair's *Statistical Account of Scotland*, dating from the 1790s, which provides a retrospective picture of many developments earlier in the eighteenth century. Apart from these and other useful documentary sources, the Galloway countryside and its heritage of buildings and other features help to form a clearer picture of a radically different landscape.

The relative backwardness which typified Scottish farming before the era of agrarian improvement was omnipresent in Galloway. Symson, writing in 1684, describes in some detail the land-use pattern of the late seventeenth century. Agricultural land, as elsewhere in Lowland Scotland, was divided into 'in-field' and 'out-field', the former worked as arable in 'run-rigg' strips, the latter largely devoted to pasture and grazing. Beyond the out-field was common grazing or moor ground, often entirely unimproved and little attended, the province of the local ferme-toun inhabitants or burgesses if the common in question lay within the bounds of a nearby burgh. Certain sophistications of husbandry and crop rotation were not entirely absent in this basic land-use pattern. A four-fold rotational system, described by Symson, was apparently common to much of Galloway, the land of a ferme-toun (or group of farmsteads) being divided into eight fields.

Only four would be worked in any year, while the remainder lay fallow, to be used as seasonal grazing like the out-field or moor beyond the run-riggs. The four cropped fields were described as follows:

Lay   the field where the beasts were folded the summer before
Awell   the field where the beasts were folded the last but one
Third Cropt   the field where the beasts were folded two years before
Fourth Cropt   the field 'little cultivated by good husbandmen'

Oxen and horses were used at the plough and the main crop was oats, grown in the 'oatland'. 'In some places near the sea', wrote Symson, 'a whiter corn is grown', and some of this exported, probably the earliest reference to the grain trade which became so significant to Galloway in the late eighteenth and early nineteenth centuries. Flax for domestic use was cultivated in the 'hemp-rigg' and the other important food grain was 'beir', a coarse grain resembling modern oats, but used then like barley.

Husbandry in Galloway seems in some respects to have been in advance of the rest of Scotland, including the rich arable lands of Fife and the Lothians. Lands adjoining the sea-shore benefited not only from fertilising with wrack or seaweed but also from liming, shells being burnt on the shore in primitive kilns fired with peats. Yet, although it is possible to detect advances in arable practice, the most radical developments were undoubtedly taking place in pasture farming, for which Galloway has since been well known. The origins of large-scale cattle pasturage in the Province can be traced back to the sixteenth century, for Hector Boece, a contemporary traveller, described the districts as having 'store of bestiall', and other commentators wrote about the growth of cattle grazing and droving trade during the seventeenth century.

With the natural environmental advantages of fine pastures and relative proximity to English markets, it is perhaps not surprising that the more enterprising lairds of the time turned their attention to the cattle trade. Success clearly depended on a number of critical factors. Firstly, there was the need to build up herds of good stock, which meant paying attention to selection and breeding, virtually unknown till that time. Secondly, landowners had to provide safe pasturage, where beasts might graze unmolested, for fattening before the long drove south. Thirdly, the successful pursuit of the cattle trade required easy access to meat markets in

England, and reliable cattle drovers to see the stock there safely. It was for these reasons, and above all the profitability of the trade, that Galloway lairds and nobles, and through them the Scottish Parliament, began in the late seventeenth century to concern themselves with the enclosing of land for pasture, and the fixing and maintaining of traditional drove roads through the wild countryside of the South West to Dumfries and by Solway Sands or Sark Bridge over the Western March to England.

The major pioneer of the cattle trade was Sir David Dunbar of Baldoon, who began to enclose land in the Machers of Wigtownshire for grazing during the last quarter of the seventeenth century. A contemporary account records:

> Sir David Dunbar of Baldone hath a park about two miles and an half in length and ane mile and a half in breadth, the greatest part whereof is rich and deep valley ground and yields excellent grass. This park can keep in it winter and summer about a thousand bestaill, part of which he buys from the countrey, and grazeth there all winter, the other part whereof is of his own breed.

Dunbar was also involved in the illicit importation of Irish cattle, which later became a major element in the Galloway trade. Once shipped ashore, beasts were fattened in the enclosed parks before droving south. With other lairds, Dunbar petitioned the Privy Council in 1697 to appoint a Commission of the Scottish Parliament 'to make and mark a road and highway for droves from New Galloway to Dumfries, holding the high and accustomed travelling way betwix the two said Burghs'. Local farmers, of course, had no love of the droves, for crops growing in unfenced fields were often injured by passing herds.

Lord Basil Hamilton, who inherited Dunbar's estates by marriage, undertook further improvements before his death in 1701, and other Galloway lairds were not slow to appreciate the monetary advantages of the 'new system' of agriculture. By the second decade of the eighteenth century, enclosures were becoming less and less objects of curiosity. Sir Thomas Gordon of Earlston, for example, erected 'a stone fence' four miles long on his property, enclosing a substantial grazing park, and elsewhere in both the Stewartry and Wigtownshire dyke building proceeded apace.

The reaction on the part of tenant farmers to this new wave of enclosure was perhaps predictable, for the first step of the 'improving' landlords was the serving of notices of eviction from the lands concerned. The origins of the Levellers' Rising can be seen in just such a series of events early in 1723. Notices to quit at Whitsunday were served on a large number of tenants in the Stewartry, and soon afterwards these men banded together to discuss tactics at Keltonhill Fair. The leadership of the movement during the early days of the Rising seems to have been in the hands of a man named Robertson, a tenant of Sir Thomas Gordon, and another man deprived of his lands by Lady Mary Kenmure. The principal complaint voiced by the Levellers during 1723 was undoubtedly the dominating issue of enclosure, especially of common grazing lands, although controversy later arose over leases and rents.

Popular protest was not by any means new to Galloway. Throughout the seventeenth century the area had been a hot-bed of Covenanting activity (see Chapter Four) generated as much by political motives as religious ideals. Perhaps the most remarkable aspect of the Levellers' Rising was the interest and involvement of such establishment figures as clergy and lesser landowners. Although neither group could be described as leaders of the movement, they were certainly active participants on the fringes. Moreover, the Rising itself had clear religious and political undertones, or at least it was construed that way by the authorities. Wild rumours of a mass rising provoked by Irish Jacobites or religious zealots were part and parcel of the contemporary reports, which caused widespread concern both in Galloway and beyond. The picture presented by observers during the spring and summer of 1724 is a particularly confused one, and naturally enough commentators like the Earl of Galloway, a leading landowner fearing for his estates and cattle, were hardly likely to be unbiased. Likewise press reports are extremely unreliable, are laced with vitriolic outbursts against the activities of the Levellers and give little positive indication of the timing of events. It is this latter factor and the weird mixture of fact and fantasy which lends to the whole affair a considerable element of mystery.

There is little mystery, however, about the general course of the Rising during 1724-5, even though it is extremely difficult to fill in the details of chronology and the personalities involved. The first news of the Levellers was reported in the *Caledonian Mercury* of 21 April:

Page 53
(*Above left*) The Old Town
House and Tolbooth,
Kirkcudbright, once the
gaol for witches, Coven-
anters and Levellers;
(*above right*) the Tolbooth
door and steps, showing
the Town Cross and well
beneath. Note the 'jougs'
or iron collar for wrong-
doers; (*left*) Title page
from *A New Confutation
of Sadducism*

Page 54
Portraits by Allan Ramsay:
(*left*) Lady Catherine
Murray; (*below*) the
Hon Admiral Keith
Stewart

The Agrarian Revolution and the Levellers

We are credibly informed from Galloway and other places in the West, that a certain Mountain Preacher, in a Discourse he had in that District not many Days ago, among other Things, so bitterly inveighed against the Heritors and others of that Country, for their laudable Frugality in Inclosures etc and (as he term'd it) making Commonty Property, that next Morning several Hundred arm'd Devotees, big with that ancient *Levelling* Tenet, in a few Hours rid themselves of that Grievance, to the great Detriment of the Gentlemen in the Neighbourhood.

By this time the ejected tenants had organised themselves in the fight against the landowners, gaining the support of the peasantry in many parts of Galloway, but above all in the Stewartry parishes of Twynholm, Tongland, Kelton and Crossmichael, where numerous dykes were attacked and levelled by night. Soon the Rising spread, and when the first public statement of the Levellers' grievances and objectives was published it was fixed to the kirk doors of Twynholm, Tongland and Borgue, showing that the focus of activities lay firmly in the Dee Valley. The Rev James Menteith of Borgue was one of several ministers who openly voiced support for the Levellers, and it is likely that he or one of his colleagues was the 'Mountain Preacher' described in the *Caledonian Mercury*'s first report.

The Rising had gathered further momentum by the beginning of May and several large bands roamed Galloway in levelling raids. One of the largest, over a thousand strong, started out from Keltonhill (centre of a famous fair and an important gathering place for cattle drovers), working its way south to Kirkcudbright, where a declaration of loyalty to Crown and Government was proclaimed and discussions held between the leaders and local gentry. But the mob did not disperse, left the town and cut back to Kelton. They were only persuaded to pass dykes by undisturbed and ultimately disband at Tongland through the efforts of the Rev William Falconer, a local clergyman sympathetic to their cause. An alarmed Earl of Galloway wrote from Glasserton to his brother-in-law Sir John Clerk of Penicuik on 2 May with news of another large group 'eight or nine hundred and most of them armed', which was rumoured to be intent on demolishing 'all Parks upon the Watter of Cree'. Galloway added that 'we shall not onlie lose our encloasours but are in hazard of losing our stocks, having noe fences for them and most goe adrift through the whole countrie'.

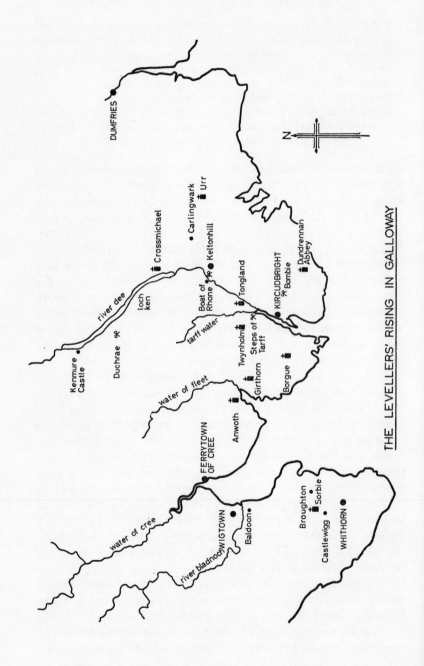

THE LEVELLERS' RISING IN GALLOWAY

The Agrarian Revolution and the Levellers

Though the Earl of Galloway's report would seem to indicate a movement westward, the focus of discontent remained firmly in the Stewartry. The Levellers had begun to step up activities and, by 6 May, James Clerk, Collector of Customs at Kirkcudbright, could report to his brother Sir John, in Edinburgh, that 'they have already thrown down about 12 or 14 gentlemen's inclosures, and are still going on'. The day before, 5 May, a major confrontation between the Levellers and a group composed of lairds and JPs led by the Stewart-Depute, the senior law officer for Kirkcudbright, had taken place at Steps of Tarf on the river Dee, north of the town. The gentry, seeing a thousand men 'armed in front with 300 good effective firelocks, the rest with pitch forks and clubs, and all with resolution enough', and knowing the weakness of their position without the backing of troops, negotiated with the mob, Patrick Heron, a landowner from the western Stewartry, representing them.

During the rest of May, and despite condemnation of their activities by Kirkcudbright Presbytery, by ministers, lesser landowners and townsfolk sympathetic to their cause, and by the General Assembly of the Church of Scotland meeting in Edinburgh, the Levellers continued their attacks on dykes and enclosed parks, seizing and generally slaughtering any cattle thought to be imported from Ireland contrary to Act of Parliament. Hurriedly assembled local troops, mostly drawn from the Earl of Stair's Dragoons, managed to track down and arrest some of the movement's leaders, including the man Robertson and David Rae, who was later committed to prison in Edinburgh. Large bands of dyke breakers—up to 2,000 strong—confronted the authorities at Bombie Moor on the 12th and at Keltonhill, a favourite rallying point, on the 26th. They ventured forth from these meetings on levelling raids throughout the neighbourhood. The support of local peasantry was sought by proclamations at churches, one on 10 May being read in eight parishes and another on 31 May announced in twelve kirks, events which presumed widespread sympathy if not support by at least some local clergy.

Meantime more troops arrived in Kirkcudbright, drawn from the locality and from Edinburgh: six troops of dragoons were reported by the *Caledonian Mercury* on 2 June to have left the city for the west, 'the better to Level the Levellers'. The combined force was under the command of Major du Cary, who was to play an important role in negotiation with the Levellers and in crushing the leadership of the Rising during June.

The first major sortie by the augmented force against the Levellers took place on 2 June when du Cary set out from Kircudbright with two troops of horse and four of dragoons, accompanied by sundry local gentry. The military were set to confront the mob at Boat of Rhone near Keltonhill, but it was not until later the same day that the two sides actually met at Steps of Tarf, further downstream. There, a tiny force of Levellers, a mere fifty strong, was soon dispersed, many being taken prisoner. Despite further arrests, the dyke levelling continued, for the *Caledonian Mercury* could report on 16 June that:

> We hear the Levellers begin again to peep out since the Forces are retir'd to their Quarters; and lest the work should not be regularly carried on, they in the Night time detach some *chosen ones* into the Country, who soon remove all Objects of Offence, and bring all to a beloved Parity. We see here handed about a very scriptural printed Three-halfpenny Apology for these Men, pretending to justice this their Procedure with the Square of the Sacred Text.

The tailpiece refers to a pamphlet entitled *News from Galloway*, which circulated widely in southern Scotland. It was generally sympathetic to the aims of the Rising, but was mysteriously laced with religious justifications, suggesting that it may have been the work of one of the clergy active on the fringes of the movement.

The Rising was not completely crushed that summer and outbursts of dyke breaking continued well into the autumn, both in Kirkcudbright and Wigtown. The last major stand of the Stewartry Levellers took place at Duchrae in the parish of Balmaghie, and many arrests followed. Yet still the levelling went on sporadically and as late as 18 November Brigadier John Stewart of Sorbie could write:

> Since my last they have not been soe violent upon the dicks in genll, but the spirett keeps upp amongst them. They, one Wednesday night last, mett in a considerable body near Whithorne with sythes, pithfforks [*sic*] and other wapons, killed and houghed Wig's cattle in the inclosure they lately throen doun, but being advertised from the toun that the dragoons were mounting to march upon them they dispersed and severalls of them threw away ther wapons which have been since found. They have break to pieces severall of my brother's big yetts upon highways, leading through his inclosures to Whithorne,

THE
Caledonian Mercury:
BEING,

An Account of all the moſt conſiderable NEWS *Foreign* and *Domeſtic*.

Edinburgh, April 21. We hear from good Hands, that there are private Letters in Town, bearing, that the Parliament was to have been adjourned as on Wedneſday laſt.

Laſt Week the Right Honourable the Earl of March, and ſome other Perſons of Diſtinction, came to Town.

We are credibly informed from Galloway and other Places in the Weſt, That a certain Mountain Preacher, in a Diſcourſe he had in that Diſtrict not many Days ago, among other Things, ſo bitterly inveighed againſt the Heritors and others of that Country, for their laudable Frugality in Incloſures, &c. and (as he term'd it) making Commonty Property, that next Morning ſeveral Hundred arm'd Devotees, big with that ancient *Levelling* Tenet, in a few Hours rid themſelves of that Grievance, to the great Detriment of the Gentlemen in the Neighbourhood.

Had our Religioſo been as ſolicitous in enforcing the Doctrines of Love and Peace, and of ſuffering (even Injuries) rather than ſin, 'tis a Queſtion if his Rhetoric had ſo readily obtain'd.

We hear there is a Woman now in Dyſart Priſon, for barbarouſly cutting the Throat of a Child of three Years old near that Place.

Haddingtoun, April 24, 1724.

Beſt Wheat, L. 8. ſh. 12.	2d *Ditto,* L. 08. ſh. 06.	3d. *Ditto,* L. 08. ſh. 00
Beſt Bear, L. 8. ſh. 14.	2d *Ditto,* L. 08. ſh. 12.	3d *Ditto,* L. 08. ſh. 08
Beſt Oats, L. 6. ſh. 15.	2d *Ditto,* L. 06. ſh. 12.	3d *Ditto,* L. 06. ſh. 10
Beſt Peaſe, L. 7. ſh. 12.	2d *Ditto,* L. 07. ſh. 08.	3d *Ditto,* L. 07. ſh. 06.

ADVERTISEMENTS.

§✝§ *That the good Ship, call'd,* The MARY of Leith, *Alexander Ogilvie Maſter, as ſhe preſently lies in the Harbour of Leith, with her whole Furniture, Burden 32 Tons, or thereby, is to be expoſed to voluntary Roup and Sale, in the Houſe of William Brown, on the Coal-hill of Leith, upon Friday the firſt of May next, betwixt the Hours of Two and Four in the Afternoon. The Inventaries of the ſaid Ship to be ſeen at the Exchange Coffee-houſe in Edinburgh, and Will's Coffee-houſe in Leith.*

Extract from the *Caledonian Mercury*, 21 April 1724

and they have breack and destroyed almost all the cariages and tools Broughton had for making up his inclosures. They have likewise a practise in sending ther emissaries in the night time to the country peoples houses, threatning them that iff they doe not join them to burn ther houses and meal stacks.

Early the following year prosecutions took place and heavy fines were imposed on those involved in the Rising and unlucky enough to be apprehended. The degree of local sympathy among merchants and lesser gentry seems to have done much to reduce the severity of the law.

So ended a short-lived but dramatic outburst of popular reaction against agrarian change in south-west Scotland. The Rising of the Levellers undoubtedly affected the course of the Agrarian Revolution in Galloway, by slowing down for a time the enclosure of grazing land and resulting in a slower growth of the cattle trade. Indirectly too it may have contributed to the rise of market-orientated arable farming, for the region became an important exporter of grain in the latter half of the eighteenth century. Yet there can be no question that Galloway was in the vanguard of agricultural change and was in an excellent geographical situation to exploit at any future time markets on all coasts of the Irish Sea. The legacy of the Levellers' Rising certainly tempered the rate and character of change in the countryside. By the middle of the eighteenth century a group of truly enlightened landowners, like James Murray of Broughton and Cally, or William Craik of Arbigland, had emerged, who were interested as much in the welfare of their tenantry as in the growth of their personal fortunes and estates. The men who learned the lessons of this remarkable incident went on to create with foresight and humanity the present-day landscape of Galloway.

References for this chapter are on pages 160–1

CHAPTER SIX

The landscape of improvement

The two major features of the eighteenth-century landscape of improvement in agriculture were the planned
village and country house, both generally associated
with a nearby estate. The landed gentleman interested in better
techniques of husbandry and agricultural development was also
likely to be concerned with more general economic growth. It
seemed to him a logical step from an improved agriculture,
bringing higher yields and profits, to investment of any surplus in
primary processing industries, such as brewing, tanning and textiles, or in turnpike roads and shipping to carry his products to
market. Another desirable objective was a settled rural population,
whether for reasons of political and physical control or even
genuine philanthropy. Many landlords sought the solution to the
problems of a tenantry displaced by agricultural improvements,
of the need to maintain a skilled labour force in the countryside,
and the desire to develop a more balanced economy linking farming with rural industry, in the creation of villages where these aims
might be attained. Landed gentlemen also sought the prestige
brought by enhancing the family patrimony with a country seat
appropriate to their status. Later they might add a wing or two
and have the surrounding countryside landscaped into an ornamental park with plantations and a water feature, such as a lake.
The outstanding example of this phenomenon in Galloway is
undoubtedly that created by James Murray of Cally (see Chapter
Eight) at Gatehouse-of-Fleet, but there are numerous others
throughout the length and breadth of the Province, from Kirkpatrick-Durham in the east to Port Logan in the Rhinns of
Galloway. Moreover, there are countless villages, built in the
period 1770–1830, that were either purely agricultural in origin or
combined agriculture and rural industry, as well as those that

grew up along turnpike roads or at ports and harbours by Solway shore. The wide range of country houses and estates included that associated with Castle Douglas, a dramatic mock-Gothic edifice called Gelston Castle completed for Sir William Douglas during 1797–8. At the other extreme was Monreith House near Port William, the modest home of the local landowning family of Maxwell.

PLANNED VILLAGES

Before the eighteenth century, Galloway was almost wholly rural in character, the main urban settlements being medieval burghs which had never grown into places of much consequence. The earliest were Dumfries (1186), at the gateway to the Province, and the ports of Wigtown (1292) and Kirkcudbright (1330), all royal burghs. Of similar origin were later burghs with charters from crown, church or local nobility: Whithorn (1325), Stranraer (1617), New Galloway (1630) and Newton Stewart (1677), some combining the defensive function with that of market place for a limited hinterland. The increased prosperity following in the wake of economic development in the latter half of the eighteenth century revitalised many of the old burghs as centres of trade and commerce, especially the ports like Kirkcudbright, Wigtown and Stranraer. In the surrounding countryside an increasingly rationalised agriculture meant the demise of scattered crofts and farmsteads, and the concentration of labour either in tied cottages adjoining the new, larger farmsteads or in planned villages or small towns, deliberately created by 'improving' landowners. These new settlements were of three main types: the formal, planned villages, like Gatehouse, Castle Douglas and Kirkpatrick-Durham (see Appendix 3); the informal period villages, such as Dalbeattie, Kirkcowan or Sorbie; and, lastly, communication villages built along turnpikes or at harbours, for example, Palanackie, Port William and Glenluce.

The earliest and most significant single eighteenth-century development in Galloway was Gatehouse-of-Fleet, which today presents 'a rare and beautiful example of an arrested industrial village and a source of satisfaction for the industrial archaeologist'. James Murray of Cally planned and directed the building of Gatehouse after 1765 and successfully established there a wide range of craft and processing industries, including tanneries,

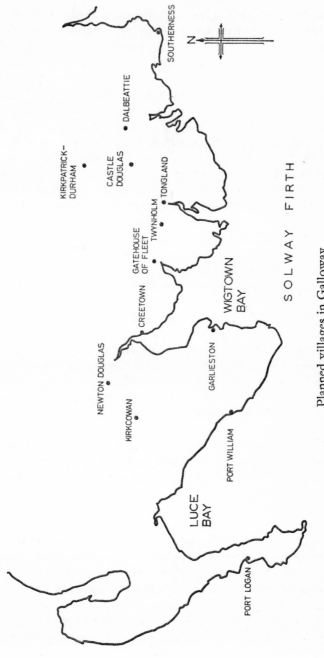

SOUTHERNESS

DALBEATTIE

KIRKPATRICK–
DURHAM

CASTLE
DOUGLAS

TONGLAND

TWYNHOLM

GATEHOUSE
OF FLEET

CREETOWN

NEWTON DOUGLAS

KIRKCOWAN

GARLIESTON

WIGTOWN
BAY

PORT WILLIAM

SOLWAY FIRTH

LUCE
BAY

PORT LOGAN

N

Planned villages in Galloway

breweries and a soapworks. The growth of textiles, and especially cotton spinning using water power, was a logical extension of these activities and in 1785 Murray granted Messrs Birtwhistle & Sons of Yorkshire, an old established firm of cattle-dealers and merchants, a lease of land on the banks of the Fleet. A joint-stock company, in which Murray held shares, was formed and soon after built 'a large fabric at Great expense' on land immediately upstream of Fleet Bridge. They followed this with a second mill and a Mr McWilliam established a third in the same complex. Thomas Scott & Co (an Ulster concern) built a fourth cotton mill on the north-east side of the village adjacent to the entrance to Cally Park. Water to drive these mills—and the several other industries of Gatehouse—was brought to the village by an extensive system of lades from Loch Whinyeon, located four miles away in the hills above the Fleet valley. The main lade cost £1,200 and supplied dams at the head of the village with 'copious streams of water'. From these dams two lades carried water to the various mills. One passed through the centre of the village, serving a brass foundry, a brewery, and the two large wheels of the Birtwhistle mills, which according to the *Factory Return* of 1839 produced 55hp between them. The other lade followed the eastern edge of the village, powering Scott's mill and one of Gatehouse's two tanneries. Although the majority of industries in Gatehouse did not survive the half-century mark, and its canal and harbour at Port Macadam were moribund by 1900, much of the original planned village survives providing a veritable paradise for the latent industrial archaeologist.

Two modern communities which had common origins as eighteenth-century planned industrial villages, developed by William Douglas the merchant-landowner (see Chapter Eight), are Newton Stewart and Castle Douglas. The former had earlier been raised to the status of burgh of barony, but in reality had never been anything more than a 'parchment burgh' before being acquired by William Douglas as part of an estate deal in the early 1780s. When Robert Heron visited Newton Douglas (as it became when Douglas had its charter renewed) in 1792 he found 'a thriving village of late origin' with a population of 1,000, where 'an enlightened and spirited landholder' had developed the cotton textile industry. 'Since its having succeeded so happily at Gatehouse,' he wrote, 'machines for carding cotton wool have been introduced . . . and several mules for spinning cotton have been set up.' Douglas encouraged a significant range of related industries, including carpet making and handloom weaving, but not long after his death the impetus to further growth was lost and Newton Douglas reverted both to its former name and function— as market centre for the Cree valley and post-town on the Carlisle–Portpatrick Turnpike. Carlingwark, a small estate and village situated on the old military road beside Carlingwark Loch, was purchased by William Douglas in 1789 and the following year he obtained a charter erecting it into a burgh of barony called Castle Douglas. He then began the creation of a classical planned village, with gracious and widely spaced streets running at right angles to each other, in the best traditions of Georgian town-planning. Robert Burns poured scorn on the Douglas family for, as he put it, 'christening towns far and near', and there is little doubt that William at any rate hankered after the prestige this brought. The astute Robert Heron, on the other hand, was kinder, remarking in his *Observations* that 'this village every day becomes more thriving and respectable; flax dressers, weavers, tanners, saddlers, masons and carpenters are now established', the last two trades no doubt being employed in building the new houses of Castle Douglas. William Douglas turned his new town into the commercial heart of the Stewartry and, although few of the industries he established there were to survive long, Castle Douglas grew into a bustling market town, which even today retains much of the period charm envisaged by its creator.

A more modest example of the integrated estate-planned village was developed five miles north-east of Castle Douglas at Kirkpatrick-Durham by that redoubtable enthusiast for agricultural improvement, the Rev Dr David Lamont. In 1774, at the age of twenty-one Lamont, whose forebears were lesser landowners, was ordained to Kirkpatrick-Durham. After inheriting three nearby estates he became extensively involved in local government affairs and a leading exponent of agricultural change and economic development. Lamont began his village at Kirkpatrick-Durham in 1785, and in his own words 'brought a livelieness and animation to the place'. The little village street soon had fifty dwellings, with a further fifty planned, and a number of modest crafts and industries, including several run by 'small societies of industrious men', who were encouraged in their efforts by the paternal

The old Town House and steeple, Castle Douglas

Lamont. By 1811 Kirkpatrick-Durham's population had risen to
1,150, sported seven inns and ale-houses, and a course on which
horse races were regularly run. Dr Lamont built his own house
near the village at Durhamhill and for nearly half a century interested himself in local affairs and the work of the church, becoming
Moderator of the General Assembly of the Church of Scotland in
1822. His village survives to the present day almost as he must
have known it.

Another settlement laid out on classical Georgian lines and with
some fine period architecture is the planned port village of Garlieston, begun before 1790 by John, Lord Garlies. It was described
about this time as 'a considerable village of recent erection . . .
pleasantly built in the form of a crescent along the head of a
bay . . . and an excellent fishing station'. Like Gatehouse, the village of Garlieston, with its modest industries and seafaring community, was a logical extension of the massive estate improvement
undertaken by the Earls of Galloway in the surrounding parish of
Sorbie. According to the *Statistical Account* (1791) the landscape
before 1765 was 'almost in a state of nature' and a radical transformation had been brought about in under thirty years. Later the
harbour itself was greatly extended and Garlieston by the early
1800s had become one of the most important ports in the Machers
district, having its own vessels trading to London, Liverpool,
Dublin and Glasgow. *Pigot's Commercial Directory of Scotland* for
1825–6 (an invaluable tool for the economic and social historian)
lists among the trades of Garlieston shipbuilding, rope and sail-
making and shows the dominance of maritime activities there.
Despite the arrival on the scene in 1876 of the Wigtownshire
Railway and the construction of a tramway extension to the
harbour, Garlieston, like nearby Port William, retained something
of its sea-going trade. Today the harbour is deserted, save for the
odd fishing boat. Garlieston and the nearby policies of Galloway
House (now a residential school) provide another outstanding
example of the eighteenth-century 'improved' estate and its
associated planned village.

There are numerous examples of less 'formal' villages created
by local landowners during the closing decades of the eighteenth
century. The majority had all the characteristics of villages like
Gatehouse, save the ordered symmetry of a grid-iron ground
plan. The best Stewartry examples are Dalbeattie, begun c 1781 by

its co-founders Alexander Copland and George Maxwell, and Creetown, established as a burgh of barony some ten years later by James McCulloch of Barholm. Dalbeattie was by far the larger, with a significant port at Dub o'Hass (the head of navigation on the Urr), several textile and paper mills, and a country forge, all driven by water power. Creetown, which like Dalbeattie was to become a centre of granite quarrying in the nineteenth century, owed its initial growth to an important ferry point on the Cree, afterwards acquiring a lead shot mill (processing lead from nearby Blackcraig mines), a small cotton mill and several other crafts. Textile manufacture was a common link between two of Wigtownshire's many Georgian villages: Kirkcowan on the Tarff Water probably grew in importance after 1790 under the patronage of John and Robert Milroy, founders of nearby cotton and woollen mills; and, further west in the Rhinns of Galloway, Stoneykirk, a centre of flax growing and coarse linen yarn production, where according to the *Statistical Account* (1792) there were four flax mills and a bleachfield.

The growth of communications, and especially turnpike roads and harbours, in the latter half of the eighteenth century led to the development of many new communities and the revitalisation of older villages throughout the length and breadth of Galloway. Glenluce, with its fine period domestic architecture, shops and old inns, is one among several good turnpike examples, including those, like Crocketford or Bridge of Dee, which grew up at change-houses, toll-bars, road-junctions or bridges. The harbour villages are almost too numerous to mention (see Chapter Eleven), but perhaps the most surprising is Palnackie on the upper reaches of the Urr estuary. It became the centre of the Urr's seafaring community and is still an active harbour, despite the extremes of tide which are such a hazard to navigation everywhere in the Solway Firth. Even after the coming of the railway the Solway was the economic lifeline of many coastal communities, especially those of southern Wigtownshire. One harbour that was of critical importance in the Machers district was Port William. Sir William Maxwell of Monreith founded and gave his name to this small port village c 1776, and some twenty years later it was described as 'a small neat village, consisting of low houses, well built, facing the sea'. The harbour was extended in the early decades of the nineteenth century and as late as World War I two-masted trading sloops tied up there. Like nearby Isle of Whithorn, Port William has recovered some of its former liveliness and is used by the occasional fishing boat and sailing yacht.

In many respects the period village, whether formally planned or not, is the most tangible element of the eighteenth-century heritage in Galloway. Nearly two hundred years after their creation, the majority survive as active communities—a very real tribute to the men of vision who brought them into being.

COUNTRY HOUSES

The country house effectively emphasises the immense contrast between the gloom of seventeenth-century Galloway and the prosperity and optimism which characterised the second half of the eighteenth century. Indeed the formal planned architecture can be regarded as a conscious expression by country gentlemen of this new confidence, order and security. The plans and principles used in their buildings were derived from English architectural pattern books containing specimen plans, such as W. Halfpenny's *The Country Gentlemen's Pocket Companion and Builder's Assistant*, from portfolio collections of prints of English country seats, from books dealing with antiquarian research and the buildings of classical antiquity, and also from the experience of Galloway gentlemen on regular treks to London, France and Italy. It is interesting that Mylne's letter (see Appendix 3c) also dealt with the cameos, portraits, 'mandolines and musick' he was collecting in Rome for Lord Garlies.

The same theories of correctness, proportions and good taste that were used in building large country houses were also applied to the design on a smaller scale of farm buildings, town and village houses, manses and churches. The architects were almost certainly local builders working from pattern-book plans, preparing designs, estimates and contracts, and generally following the whole process through to completion. Much of the work was certainly of a very high standard, and it does seem that lack of formal training in architecture and aesthetic appreciation was of little significance. At the same time after the 1750s local men, working as land surveyors, mapmakers and estate managers, planned the geometrically divided, dyked, ditched and fenced landscape around these houses. Some, like Patrick Stewart (1734–1814), working for the Stair and Galloway estates, were surveyors, farm managers and themselves small proprietors. Others—like John Gillone, working in the Kirkcudbright area in the 1770–80s for the Cally and Galloway estates and for Kirkcudbright burgh, and William Dunbar of Creebridge, Newton Stewart, working in Wigtown-shire in the 1790s and 1800s—were primarily mapmakers, as well as being planners. Some superb examples of their work are contained in the Broughton and Cally Muniments and the Agnew Papers in the Scottish Record Office. These estate papers also include a few contracts and plans for various buildings and smaller houses. Other useful sources include the William Roy maps (c 1747–55), which give detailed pictures of estate planning round the great houses, like Castle Kennedy and Castlewigg (see plate on p 18), and the John Ainslie maps of the Stewartry (1796) and of Wigtownshire (1782); travellers' descriptions of their domestic 'grand tours'; Statistical Account material, in particular for Gir-thon, Whithorn, Glasserton and Sorbie parishes; and for colourful background evidence the prints from watercolours by William Daniell in Galloway in 1816 and by John Clark in the 1820s.

Although the centrepiece of each estate was, of course, the great man's house, as at Kirkdale, Cally, Glasserton, Galloway House, Castle Kennedy, Castlewigg, in fact most landowners paid as much attention to the surrounding landscape. The development of formal gardens on a large scale dates back to the last quarter of the seventeenth century. Sir John Clerk of Penicuik, who had married Lady Margaret Stuart, a sister of the 5th Earl of Galloway in 1701, describes splendid displays at ducal seats and small lairds' houses as early as 1721. At Drumlanrig the gardens were 'excellently laid out in the newest fashion with parterrs, tarasses, sloping banks, wildernesses, hedges, waterworks . . . dayly at work a gardiner and 26 men to dress them'; at Bargaly, Andrew Heron had established 'gardens, orchards, parterrs, orangeries, water works, fishponds, bagnios, inclosures, arbures, wildernesses, woods . . .'. The bagnios or hot-houses at Cally in the 1790s produced apricots, figs, nectarines and grapes. Probably the most elaborate gardens were those at Castle Kennedy, with avenues converging on a pond like a giant wheel. They were restored after 1840.

By the later eighteenth century a whole language of the pic-turesque and sublime was being applied to landscapes with grace-

Page 71 (*Above*) Lochryan House, near Stranraer c 1890, by George Washington Wilson, the pioneer Scottish photographer; (*below*) Kirkdale House from the south

Page 72 Kirkpatrick-Durham, a typical planned village of the late eighteenth
century, developed by the local landowner, the Rev Dr David Lamont

ful woodland rides, avenues, heronries and deer parks, artificial ponds and lakes, bridges and roads. At Cally 'every deformity within these grounds is concealed, or converted into a beauty by wood'. Stables, home farms, dairies, laundries, chapels, icehouses and dovecots were regarded as being both functional and decorative. Follies, temples and fashionable ruins were added as special points of interest—a 'Gothic' temple built in 1778–9 on Cally estate 'to accidental observation has all the effect that might be produced by a genuine antique'.

Among the more interesting country houses in different parts of Galloway are Goldilea (931735), Greenlaw (754644) and Barwhinnock (656549), and, with the removal of nineteenth-century additions, Physgill (428367) and Logan (096428). Cally House (600549) and its policies are of outstanding interest; the house, now a hotel, was built to plans by Robert Mylne for James Murray in 1763, but was considerably altered with massive additions including a portico and wings in 1835. The policies include private roads and bridges, an artificial lake, impressive estate walls, a splendid stable block (603552), Cally Mains farm (592542), and the Temple (606543), a two-storey 'ecclesiastical' folly.

Kirkdale House (514533), built 1780–7 to plans by Robert Adam (the original drawings are in the Sir John Soane collection), is probably the finest house in Galloway. The symmetrically fronted, four-storey, grey granite centre block, with three-storey wings on each side, is unaltered externally (see plate on p 71). It was built by Sir Samuel Hannay (1742–90), a Galloway laird with a career behind him as a chemist and drug merchant in London, who had extensive trading, financial and shipping interests. He was also MP for Camelford in Cornwall (1784–90). The earlier octagonal stable block (512536), further up the hill, consisting of four two-storey buildings linked by single-storey wings, is a superb composition. Further up the hill again in Kirkdale churchyard (512541) is the granite mausoleum erected by Hannay in 1787. Kirkdale bridge, near the entrance to the house, was also built c 1785–90 to an Adam plan. The charming circular domed icehouse, with its small forecourt (516530)—just below the A75 road—was formerly built into the escarpment of Kirkdale Burn nearer the bridge. In the gorge below is Kirkdale Bank mote, marked as 'The World's End' on a 1761 map. Though now overgrown and dangerous, it was landscaped with walks and stone

E

causeways to a small summer house on top. The feature commonly known as 'Dick Hatterick's Cave' (518526), in the bank above the shore, 200yd east of the burn, rather than the smuggler's cave it is usually assumed to be, was developed by Hannay as a folly. Hannay at any rate was the kind of rascal, a large-scale gambler with a sense of taste and humour, who might have enjoyed a little practical joke of this type. The very attractive small house at Ravenshall (523523) was also built by him as a private retreat from Kirkdale.

Kirroughtree House (422660) near Minnigaff, built in 1719 by Patrick Heron, is now a hotel. The dovecot (419662), octagonal, 18ft high, with 448 nests, is an excellent example of eighteenth-century functional but decorative architecture. Galloway House (478452), near Garlieston, is interesting for the layout of its vast gardens, grounds, paths and driveways, lodges and entrance gates; the house itself is dignified but dull. Only the site of Glasserton House remains, but the fine courtyard stable range (417377), the rectangular dovecot (416379), the remains of the dairy, and the nearby Glasserton church, make an interesting group of estate and parish buildings. At the other end of Wigtownshire, Lochryan House (064687) is a charming early building, which dates from 1701, although it too has many Victorian additions.

References for this chapter are on page 161

CHAPTER SEVEN

Robert Heron's Galloway

Eighteenth-century documentary material includes a vast collection of manuscripts, mostly estate papers of the major landowners in the area, like the Agnews of Lochnaw, the Earls of Stair or the Murrays of Broughton and Cally, which is invaluable for detail on family history, and the day-to-day running of country houses and estates with their associated industries. For the overall picture of Galloway at the end of the eighteenth century, however, the social and economic historian must turn inevitably to the *Statistical Account of Scotland*, edited by Sir John Sinclair in the 1790s, which covers every parish in greater or lesser detail and contains an immense range of useful information. A sub-editor of the *Statistical Account*, Robert Heron—a particularly astute observer who travelled widely in Scotland—provided an excellent complement to this work in his two-volume *Observations made in a Journey thr' the Western Counties of Scotland in the autumn of 1792*, which appeared in 1793.

Robert Heron was born near New Galloway in 1764 and, after a conventional Scottish upbringing and education, turned to the ministry and then schoolmastering in search of career. Ultimately he rejected both and set out to make his living as a writer. Apart from his *Observations*, he wrote a book about a tour of the Hebrides, a history of Scotland and the first posthumous biography of Robert Burns.

From the historian's point of view, Heron could not have chosen a more interesting period in which to record his observations. Galloway was undergoing dramatic change, in agriculture, in crafts and industry, in the whole mode and pace of life. Heron saw and commented on the impact of the agrarian and industrial revolution, and he did so with an eye for detail which makes his *Observations* a fundamental source for the social history of the region during the closing decades of the eighteenth century.

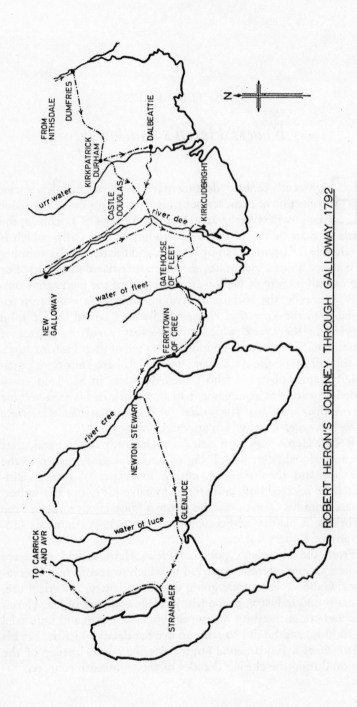

ROBERT HERON'S JOURNEY THROUGH GALLOWAY 1792

Robert Heron's Galloway

His journey into Galloway in the autumn of 1792 began at Dumfries, 'a considerable town, containing nearly 7000 inhabitants' with 'a beautiful and advantageous situation'. The place, he thought, could be described as 'a sort of metropolis', having prosperous merchants, growing industries, busy markets and harbours, a coffee house (the mark of every business centre of consequence), several banks, a printing house and a weekly newspaper:

> The amusements of this city, its advantages for education, its convenient and healthy situation, allure many of the inferior gentry from the neighbourhood to spend half, or perhaps the whole year here . . . a place of higher gaiety and elegance than any other town in Scotland of the same size.

A recently opened attraction for the landed gentlemen and the merchant *nouveaux riches* of the town was the playhouse, where 'the players fared better than in many more prosperous and opulent towns'. Communication with Galloway was being improved, for at the time of Heron's visit the 'New Bridge' to replace the old medieval one downstream was under construction.

The Rev Dr David Lamont, of Kirkpatrick-Durham (see Chapter Six), an old friend of Heron's, accompanied him on his way westwards from Dumfries. As they rode upcountry out of Nithsdale they saw 'the cornfields become less extensive, less numerous and more irregular'. 'You begin to perceive,' Heron wrote, 'that you are advancing into a country where cultivation has hardly made its way before you.' Yet the spirit of the new agriculture and of 'improvement' was in the air, with farmers becoming increasingly more market-conscious, particularly in regard to the profitable grain, sheep and black cattle trades. A short stay at Lamont's home in Kirkpatrick-Durham afforded Heron the opportunity of seeing the progress which had been made in that planned agrarian village, set above 'the highly fertile and well-cultivated' valley of the Urr.

Heron then set out for his native town of New Galloway, travelling by Castle Douglas, another rapidly expanding local community with fine period buildings in long straight streets. The town was developing successfully as a market centre in which industrial and craft activity was balanced with the farming interest of the surrounding countryside. Indeed the rural prospect in this part of Galloway was particularly prosperous:

Advancing across the ridge which divides the Dee from the Urr, I found myself in a tract of country that presented every mark of rapid improvement. The fields are divided by stone-walls of suitable height and strength. The farm houses are decently built and have their roofs commonly covered with slate. New farm houses are rising here and there . . .

and again:

All this tract of country is indeed wonderfully populous. It is a fine proof of the tendency of agriculture to bring wealth and population to those seats where it fixes. The influx of labourers from Ireland keeps the price of labour low. The vicinity of the sea-coast affords farmers sufficient convenience for the exportation of their grain. The highway leading into England gives them considerable advantages for the sale and exportation of their cattle. Hence a rapid increase of wealth and population.

New Galloway and the Glenkens district naturally receive a great deal of attention. His description of his home town still holds good today almost to the last detail:

[It] consists of two small streets, crossing each other at right angles. The houses are low, ill-built, thatched with straw, and very imperfectly repaired within. One of the streets making a part of the highway between Kirkcudbright and Dalmellington is decently paved and kept tolerably clean. The other is not usually preserved in so good condition. But, a few slate-houses, rising to the height of two stories or a storey and a half are interspersed among the lower and thatch-covered houses. The little gardens of the citizens lie close behind their houses, above and below the town: they are divided by hedges; and trees rise around, or here and there among them. The spire of the court-house is a distinguished object in the group: And when the smoke rises from the little chimneys; and the whole is viewed either from an elevation above or below, no assemblage of objects can be conceived, more pleasing to the eye and the imagination.

Much more urbane was Kirkcudbright, with its smart new streets of merchants' and lawyers' dwellings and an 'agreeable enough little circle of elegant society'. In this respect Kirkcudbright was a slightly tarnished mirror of Dumfries, being the seat of Stewartry government as well as a busy market town and customs port. A walk along Castle Street or the Old High Street will give some indication of the elegance of Georgian Kirkcudbright. But the town was also a place of everyday industry and trade, with a large population of labourers, artisans and seamen. The pubs and alehouses were probably well patronised by all classes, singing, dancing and telling tales of ghosts, fairies and witches, especially on a winter's evening.

Heron crossed the river Dee by ferry and headed towards Gatehouse-of-Fleet, riding through 'rich and fertile lands laid out either in grass-parks, or in cornfields', mostly in the rich farming neighbourhoods of Borgue and Twynholm. During the closing decades of the eighteenth century there was a dramatic spread of industry in Galloway and nowhere was this more evident than in the rapid growth of Gatehouse in the valley of the Water of Fleet. Heron devotes a great deal of space to this development, particularly the establishment of the industrial community and the living and working conditions of the people employed in Gatehouse's many trades. He extends much credit to James Murray of Broughton and Cally (see Chapter Eight) for his foresight in planning the village, and in encouraging and financing many of the crafts there. To Heron—and doubtless to other 'improvers', such as Sir John Sinclair—Gatehouse was the enlightened landed gentleman's utopia: a planned village in a rural environment with prosperous industries. These were mainly cotton spinning and weaving, but included others more closely linked with the land, such as tanning, leather-working, soap-making and brewing. Quite understandably, the growth of Gatehouse brought together a large population of artisans and labourers (the majority better provided for here than in most factory villages) and the results were not much to Heron's liking:

I wish I could honeftly add, that the morals of thefe good people have been improved with their circumftances. But proftitution and breaches of chaftity have lately become frequent here. Tippling houfes are wonderfully numerous. I was informed by the intelligent excifeman of the place, that not fewer than an hundred and fifty gallons . . of whifky alone . . had been confumed here for every week of the laft fix months. The licentioufnefs of Gatehoufe affords frequent bufinefs for the neighbouring Juftices. The Clergyman of the parifh has found it neceffary to act both as a Juftice of the Peace and as a Clergyman; and although exceedingly active in the former of thefe capacities, has yet found it too hard for him to reftrain the irregularities of thefe villagers. An affiftant has been employed to aid him in the difcharge of his clerical functions. Yet, both the pious affiduties of his affiftant, and his own labours, clerical and juridical, have proved infufficient to maintain among the manufacturers of Gatehoufe, all that purity of morals and decorum of manners which might be wifhed. It has been the great errour of the politicians and philofophers of the prefent age, that, in their care to multiply the numbers, to ftimulate the induftry, and to increafe the opulence of mankind, they have overlooked the important concern of checking their vices, and of encouraging their declining virtues.

Here is the whole debate about the consequences of industrial-isation (which still remains an obsession of the historian) seen through the eyes of a particularly observant contemporary writer.

Further to the west, beyond Anwoth and Kirkmabreck, lay Ferrytown-of-Cree, a modest granite-built village seeking to emulate Gatehouse as a centre of commerce and industry. Being a coastal village it was 'inhabited chiefly by sea-faring people' and, says Heron, 'its manners take their tone from these'. 'Here are abundance of tippling-houses,' he writes, 'but no decent or com-modious inn.' Like many harbours, and especially the isolated ones, along the Solway, Ferrytown derived no small measure of its prosperity from smuggling, largely from the Isle of Man, the contraband including 'salt, liquors, teas and a variety of East India goods imported by other European nations'. Smuggling probably provided a steadier trade than lead mining in the hills north of Creetown, though when Heron passed Machermore work was still being actively pursued by one hopeful partnership. Crossing the river Cree at Minnigaff, he arrived in the fast expand-ing village of Newton Stewart or Douglas. Here the success story of Gatehouse had been partially repeated, although William Douglas, the merchant-industrialist, had only recently acquired the estate and started to develop the old village by the introduc-tion of crafts and artisans (see Chapters Six and Eight).

Heron left Newton Douglas for Glenluce, accompanied by a Mr Hope, 'whose conversation was indeed necessary to raise my spirits above that depression which they were liable to suffer from the dreariness of the scenery . . . a wide extent of flat, bleak heath'. The road itself, however, was excellent, having recently been re-made to carry the London–Portpatrick turnpike. Another notable feature of the local landscape were the 'open' or unfenced fields, maintained 'for the accommodation of droves of Irish cattle' passing through Galloway to the English markets. At this point

Robert Heron's Galloway

Heron is very critical of the droving trade (for a full account see A. R. B. Haldane's classic book *The Drove Roads of Scotland*, 1952 reprinted 1968) saying that it brings little to the local economy and upsets not only everyday farming activities but the peace of the countryside, especially as the drovers are no respecters of the Sabbath!

Another anti-social group in Heron's eyes are the gipsies:

> Gipsy tinkers often range through these parts; selling horn spoons, smoothing irons and kettles; lodging in any barn, stable or kiln, into which they can find access; purchasing horns; and stealing provisions and cloths of all sorts . . . The gipsies are now less numerous in Galloway and other parts of Scotland, than they once were. Their manners, their trade and their traffic are everywhere the same. They keep inns; they deal in horses; and they make household utensils of horn, wood, tin, copper. Of their dress they are negligent. The intercourse of the sexes among them is promiscuous, as among the brutes: No laws of marriage are faithfully observed. They wander commonly about, in considerable bodies, averse to regular labour, and to the habits of settled life.

The days of the smugglers and the gipsies were almost over, as Galloway became less mysterious, less remote and moved increasingly into the mainstream of economic and social change.

'Near Glenluce', says Heron, 'the aspects of the country begins to soften' and 'hedges, green fields, and well-built walls of inclosure caught the eye'. He finds Glenluce itself very pleasing. The villagers in this little rural community above the valley of the Water of Luce were mostly merchants, shopkeepers, inn or alehouse keepers, labourers, artisans and sailors. Although Glenluce had no proper harbour its sea trade was growing, for 'some coasting sloops come up near to the village, entering the mouth of the little river'.

The land between Glenluce and Stranraer was well cultivated, the main crops being potatoes, oats, barley and flax, while an addition to the fattening of the ubiquitous black cattle was the feeding of swine for export to urban markets in Lancashire and the west of Scotland. On the coast salt panning was still carried on, though it was much less important than it had once been. Another seasonal occupation of local farmers was wrack or seaweed gathering, used mostly for fertilising, though on the Luce Bay shoreline some kelp making, by burning wrack, was a more profitable sideline, the product being shipped to the chemical or bleaching works to the north and south. Much of the locally grown flax was prepared in nearby mills: Stoneykirk parish had at least four water-driven 'lint' mills at the time of the *Statistical Account*, written shortly after Heron's visit. This whole district of the Rhinns of Galloway seemed to present a prosperous façade with an informal integration of agriculture and industry, such as that found in the areas around Kirkcudbright or Gatehouse.

Stranraer was Heron's last point of interest before heading north into Carrick and Ayrshire. He found here a town of 'no regular plan', where 'whole streets of new houses have lately been built', though 'still set down in a disorderly and straggling disposition'. Standing at the head of Loch Ryan, 'a noble and convenient harbour', Stranraer had an expanding sea-going trade with the Firth of Clyde, northern England and Ireland, quite apart from its modest commerce with the Baltic and West Indies. The largest single export was probably grain and meal from the surrounding farmlands of the Rhinns of Galloway. Heron seems to have spent most of his stay at Stranraer in the local coffee house arguing with some locals, 'Gentlemen of decent appearance', about such controversial topics as French democracy, Roman Catholics and Presbyterians in Ireland, and political reform in Britain. Plus ça change!

As Heron headed north along the shore of Loch Ryan he was able to see and describe the kind of things which make this closing stage of his tour in Galloway almost a microcosm of the whole trip and of the widespread changes taking place around him. At Innermessan, for example, he saw a small woollen mill and nearby a grain mill, both water-powered, and typical of so many elsewhere in the Province. Further up the coast at Cairnryan a vessel had just come from Bangor in Ulster to land cattle for droving to England and, in the hills behind, a slate quarry had been successfully worked supplying materials for local building.

So Heron closes the Galloway section of his journey through the west of Scotland, recording much more than the usual dilettante traveller's tales. His *Observations* provide a detailed pen-portrait of an economy and society undergoing change, which is of inestimable value to the historian.

References for this chapter are on page 161

CHAPTER EIGHT

Landowners and industry

Much of the history and heritage described in this book is owed to the lives and works of two eighteenth-century Gallovidians, Sir William Douglas of Gelston, the self-made merchant and entrepreneur, and James Murray of Broughton and Cally, the landowner and estate 'improver'; despite the great gulf in their social backgrounds, they would probably have taken this joint account of their activities as a compliment. They certainly shared an unbounded enthusiasm for the 'spirit of improvement' in agriculture, for transport and industrial developments, and for community building, which so changed the Galloway countryside in the eighteenth century. Douglas and Murray left their monuments not only in the communities of Newton Stewart (or Douglas), Castle Douglas and Gatehouse-of-Fleet (described in Chapter Six) which they created, but also in the surrounding countryside that once formed their estates. Like William Craik of Arbigland, the advocate of the new husbandry, Douglas and Murray were pioneers, farsighted men who saw the possibilities in the development of the natural resources of Galloway, especially its land, minerals and water-power.

They brought to late-eighteenth-century Galloway the impetus of change on the grand scale in land and industry, seeking to combine the two with a care for the environment which twentieth-century developers and planners might well emulate. Their influence on other landowners and farmers was considerable and they had many emulators in and beyond Galloway. Apart from farming and general estate management, Douglas and Murray were involved in a vast number of industrial activities, including woollen and cotton textiles, carpet weaving, tanning, leather-working, soap making and brewing. Their interests in transport developments were diverse, ranging from turnpike road building to the improvement of river navigation and ports on the Cree and the Fleet. Unquestionably a large slice of Galloway's physical landscape and industrial archaeology was created by men like Murray and Douglas. A greater insight into that heritage can clearly be gained from the lives and motives of the men who created it.

SIR WILLIAM DOUGLAS

The upbringing and early career of William Douglas remains something of a mystery for the family history is extremely sketchy and he himself had little to say of his formative years. He came of fairly well-connected landed folk, what eighteenth-century Scottish parlance would have described as 'bonnet lairds', prosperous farmers or lesser landowners. In later life, the impression given of him in contemporary letters and other records is of a hard-headed, tough-talking businessman, with plenty of personal ambition. Yet, whatever his motives, having made a fortune as a merchant in the colonial trade, he retired at an early age to his native Galloway and began an intensive programme of economic development. It is largely from the records of these activities undertaken between 1785 and his death in 1809 that the following account derives. Much of the material is to be found in correspondence in the *Melville Castle Muniments* of Henry Dundas, Scottish Secretary in the government of William Pitt, or in contemporary law suits, for Sir William Douglas, like many landowners and businessmen of the period, was never out of the courts.

Douglas, one of a large family, was born in 1745 in the parish of Penninghame and following the death of his father was brought up by an uncle. After a conventional education he in 1766 joined his older brother James, already established as a merchant in Glasgow. They later moved to London and 'entered extensively into the American trade'. The two brothers had the obvious advantage of family connections in their enterprise, for several uncles and at least two older brothers had already settled and made their fortunes in the Colonies, notably Jamaica, Virginia and in New York. Although William Douglas's lucrative partnership with his brother was formally dissolved in 1783, they maintained an informal business relationship for another six years. He then entered into association with Sir James Shaw of London, forming in 1790 the firm of Douglas & Shaw, whose active management was committed to Douglas's two co-partners, Shaw and a younger brother, Samuel. The business ability and influence of the Douglas family was clearly considerable, Sir James Shaw estimating in 1795 that the joint fortune of William Douglas and his three brothers was in the region of £400,000, discounting much of their individual wealth.

As early as 1785 the prosperous William Douglas seems 'to have resolved to retire from business and to reside on his estates in Galloway'. He wrote in these terms to his kinsmen William and John Douglas at Norfolk, Virginia, in a letter dated 22 August 1785: 'my brother James and I set off for Galloway this afternoon. We hope you will soon come over and settle in your native Country and be our neighbour lairds.' Thereafter he began to spend increasing amounts of time away from London and acquired substantial landed estates in Galloway and elsewhere, thus adding to the family patrimony in Penninghame parish. According to Sir James Shaw he possessed by the late 1790s 'considerable landed property in the neighbouring counties of Ayr and Wigtown' in addition to extensive estates in Kirkcudbright. His first major purchase was Gelston (1786) at a cost of £15,000, and to this he later added 'the small property' of Airlies in Wigtownshire (1787); Hallmyre, adjoining Gelston, purchased for £4,200 in 1788; Carlinwark (1789) costing £14,000, and Midkelton 'shortly afterwards' for an unspecified sum. Several years later, in 1796, he bought another large estate in Wigtownshire—Ardwall, the property of Major John Maxwell, which he afterwards sold. His last major purchase, in 1800, was a landed property somewhat further afield in Wales.

In the tradition of the more enlightened proprietors of the day Douglas was not simply interested in the acquisition of land, but above all in estate and agricultural 'improvement'. Where this could be combined with rural crafts or larger-scale industrial development and the harnessing of other local resources, such as water power and a flexible labour force, so much the better. It was with these aims that after the mid-1780s Douglas spent an increasing amount of the year away from London and invested a substantial part of his large fortune in promoting manufactures of different kinds in Galloway. His interests embraced the development of the two communities of Newton Douglas and Castle

Douglas; the encouragement and establishment of a wide range
of industrial enterprises, including two cotton spinning mills,
woollen and carpet mills, tanneries, breweries, domestic spinning
and handloom weaving; the construction of turnpike roads,
canals and harbours, and the creation of a country bank, of which
he was principal partner. In all but a handful of these many ventures Douglas was successful—a formidable achievement in the
space of twenty years. His personal and political influence both
within Galloway and beyond was considerable enough to provoke
the jealousy of old-established landed families. At the same time
it earned him a baronetcy—a reluctant recognition by Henry
Dundas, then Secretary for Scotland, and William Pitt, the Prime
Minister, of his power within Galloway.

William Douglas's schemes for agricultural and estate 'improvement', his support of turnpike-road and bridge-building
programmes and his interest in river navigation and canals were
widespread, but his main concerns as regards industrial development were Newton Douglas and Castle Douglas (see Chapter
Six). The most significant single industry was cotton textiles,
mainly domestic or factory spinning and handloom weaving.
According to Robert Heron, writing in 1792 after a visit to
Newton Douglas, the partnership of Douglas, Dale and McCall
planned to erect 'a large work for the spinning of cotton by mill
machinery' on the river Cree upstream from the village. Sir James
Shaw estimated that the mill, built on the west bank of the river
in 1793, cost £10,000 although later commentators put the capital
cost much higher. The site of this mill was downstream from the
present horseshoe weir, probably a reconstruction of that built to
supply the wheels of the cotton mill. About the same time
Douglas erected a 'cottonworks' at Castle Douglas, in the vicinity
of the present Cotton Street, which was described as being 'on a
smaller scale' than that at Newton Douglas. It is probable that
this second mill was nothing more than a simple factory containing hand-spinning jennies, for water-power supply would have
been a major problem in Castle Douglas. Both mills were successful enough in Douglas's own lifetime but, in the face of oncoming
general depression in the cotton trade, succumbed shortly afterwards. Unlike the larger mills at Gatehouse, those in Newton and
Castle Douglas lacking good business management never revived.

One of the most interesting and little-known schemes for regional development in which Douglas was the prime mover was the establishment in 1806 of the Galloway Banking Company (otherwise known as the partnership of Sir William Douglas, Napier & Co). For a number of years after his death this country bank was an important means of mobilising capital and providing credit to landowners, farmers and merchants in south-west Scotland. Sir James Shaw later described Douglas as the 'principal partner' of the Galloway Bank and considered it to be one of two 'great depositories of funds' belonging to him, the other being the firm of Douglas & Shaw. The Galloway Bank was a substantial concern with headquarters in Castle Douglas and agencies elsewhere in the Province. In the period of fluctuating fortunes during and after the Napoleonic Wars, when so many financial houses of similar vintage went bankrupt, the Galloway Bank managed to survive until the deep crisis of 1821. Its demise was no doubt caused by over-speculation and particularly by the associated failure of a cattle-droving firm to whom the bank had extended £55,000 credit.

The story of Douglas's elevation to a baronetcy is an interesting reflection on contemporary power politics. Having established himself as a principal landed proprietor 'laudibly employed in promoting manufactures of different kinds' and increasingly involved in local government and affairs, Douglas sought honours appropriate to his status. After constant badgering of Henry Dundas, Secretary of State, and Sir James Shaw, his business partner, he ultimately obtained his baronetcy in 1796 as Sir William Douglas of Castle Douglas. As is clear from his correspondence with Shaw, Dundas had a hard job convincing Pitt that the baronetcy was really worth the 'six *good* votes in the Stewartry and two in the Shire' which he estimated to be the extent of Douglas's 'not very considerable influence' in Galloway. Sir William coveted higher honours; he even persuaded Lord Kirkcudbright (apparently a very poor man) to part with his title and offered £30,000 to the corrupt Prince Regent to procure this title for him.

William Douglas always had the good of his native Galloway at heart, however. Not long after receiving news of his baronetcy he wrote:

> I am proud of my name and country, I have uniformly acted for the honour and interest of both; to them I chiefly owe my success in the

world and everything worthy of note I have done in it. Since I became a landed proprietor I have done all in my power to promote the prosperity of the country by encouraging improvements in agriculture, manufactures and every other kind of industry.

He certainly brought the impetus of the Industrial Revolution to the Galloway countryside and, despite the fact that few of the industries he encouraged were to survive his death, he had nevertheless made a major contribution to regional development. With customary vanity he willed himself a splendid marble tomb at a cost of £1,000. But a more significant monument is perhaps the town of Castle Douglas itself, with its classic, rectangular layout, fine period buildings, shops and old coaching inns.

JAMES MURRAY

James Murray inherited from his father, Alexander Murray (d 1750) and his mother, Lady Euphemia Stewart, daughter of the 5th Earl of Galloway, vast estates in Wigtownshire, Kirkcudbrightshire and Donegal, and an intimate connection with the leading Galloway family. His grandfather, Richard Murray of Broughton near Whithorn (d 1690), had acquired the Cally and Plunton properties through a fortuitous marriage to Anna Lennox of Cally and inherited the Killybegs estate from the 2nd Earl of Annandale. James Murray married in 1752 his 'very beautiful' cousin, Lady Catherine Stewart, daughter of the 6th Earl of Galloway. James Boswell's description is substantiated in her elegant portrait as Diana the huntress, probably by Allan Ramsay (see plate on p 54), and in the very sympathetic romantic portrait by Angelica Kauffmann, both at Cumloden. Unfortunately their only child, Alicia, died in Rome while still an infant. In 1785 James Murray astonished his relations and friends by eloping with Grace Johnston, the sister of Peter Johnston, MP for the Stewarty, and she remained with him as his mistress for the rest of his life. It was their son, Alexander, who succeeded to his estates in 1799.

James used his inheritance well, both in his own interest and for the benefit of the community as a whole. Boswell described him as an 'amiable man' with 'very good sense'. He was warm-hearted and devoted to his natural children, moderate and fair to his tenants, but at the same time tough, far-seeing, sharp even in the

Page 89
(*Above*) Print showing Gatehouse cotton mills and village c 1847; (*right*) Sir William Douglas of Castle Douglas, entrepreneur and landed gentleman

Page 90 (*Above*) Tinker gipsies at the Doon, Nunmill, near Kirkcudbright c 1900; (*below*) an old roadmender or ditcher near the harbour village of Palnackie, shown on a card posted in 1905

advancement of his financial interests, never overwhelmed by his wife's august relations and prepared to assert himself in political squabbles against their wishes. His political career, first as MP for Wigtownshire (1762-8) and then for the Stewartry of Kirkcudbright (1768-74)—after the Wigtownshire seat was passed on to his brother-in-law, Admiral Keith Stewart—was ultimately determined, however, by the Galloway interest which he represented.

His multiple activities in the management and development of his estates, in finance, banking, industry and commerce, and in politics are exceptionally well documented in the Broughton and Cally archives in the Scottish Record Office. Private papers, including letters relating to his period as a student at the University of Glasgow (1741-5), marriage contracts, and settlements on his children, and the rich and extensive estate papers, journals and plans, memoranda on the management of his estates in his absence, rental books, tacks and estate plans (eg John Gillone's *Plan of Fishing Works at Tongland 1797*) provide an excellent picture of his work on his various properties in Whithorn, Sorbie, Anwoth, Girthon, Tongland, Twynholm, Rerrick, Buittle, Borgue and Kelton parishes.

The planned town of Gatehouse-of-Fleet, laid out after 1760 on a grid pattern with parallel streets, and the fine estate policies, farms and houses remain as impressive physical evidence of Murray's imagination and good taste. The success of the industries established in his town was largely due to his initiative in providing a water supply by aqueducts and channels from Loch Whinyeon to power the tanneries and cotton mills, to his policy of generous land grants and leases to attract industrialists from outside the area—eg the contract in March 1785 dealing with the cotton mill to be established by John, Thomas and William Birtwhistle—and to his own direct participation in some ventures, such as the partnership of Borradaile Davetts & Co from 1768, with John Borradaile, tanner in Wigtown, George Atkenson, tanner in Temple Sowerby in Westmoreland, John Bushby, writer in Dumfries, and James Davetts. Under the terms of this partnership Murray derived little personal profit from the tannery. The fringe benefits included reserving for himself the right 'to have and take upon the premises from time to time . . . such part of the spent bark belonging to the Tannery as they shall have occasion for and incline to use in their Hot houses and Gardens at the Cally'.

Landowners and industry

Although it is virtually impossible to unravel the details of Murray's financial involvement with the Douglas & Heron Bank, and the profits, if any, he obtained from buying and selling landed properties, it is clear that his one main source of income was the rentals of the farms on his Galloway estates. The total annual rental of these farms in 1769 was £2,505, and this figure increased considerably over the next thirty years, as in Britain generally food prices rose, communications improved, and the markets for Galloway farm produce in the towns of central Scotland and north-west England expanded. Farming more than ever before was becoming a commercial enterprise for profit, and in turn estate management became a professional and specialised occupation, as profitable as it was interesting and time-consuming for men like James Murray, the Earls of Galloway and Stair, Lord Daer or Admiral Keith Stewart. Probably James Murray spent more time in active management and improvement of his farms than on anything else. Men of enterprise and efficiency replaced the less progressive tenants. Longer leases were granted so that farmers could participate in a shared programme of improvement, which would allow drainage, enclosure, and the new system of crop rotation. Farms were amalgamated, and new buildings and farmhouses erected everywhere on the estate. At the same time, the lesser farmers were not forgotten; Murray established small holdings in Gatehouse-of-Fleet and on a nearby farm, designed to attract settlers.

The rental book of his estates (1769–72) is a very useful volume, containing descriptions of his properties, details of the tacks and rentals, and of the obligations upon tenants and proprietor relating to farms, salmon fishings, and waulk, wheat and barley mills in Girthon, Anwoth, Tongland, Twynholm, Rerrick, Borgue, Whithorn and Sorbie parishes. The vast difference between Andrew Symson's and James Murray's Galloway is noticeable in the way the old rents in kind—in terms of loads of peats, numbers of hens, capons or chickens, stones of butter, or in days of a man's work harrowing, loading coals, or at hay or corn, all now commuted to money terms—represent only a very small, almost insignificant part of the total rentals involved.

References for this chapter are on pages 161–2

CHAPTER NINE

Politics and society in eighteenth-century Galloway

The second half of the eighteenth century was for Galloway as elsewhere in Britain an age of modernisation and
enlightenment. Although society was still essentially
dominated by a largely hereditary aristocracy, the quality of
leadership they provided was impressive. While perhaps lacking
as individuals the touch of glamour associated with contem-
poraries of humbler origin, like Robert Burns and Paul Jones,
they used their power with sense and moderation. It is perhaps
possible to paint too rosy a picture of the lives and prospects of
the working classes at that period, but it is probably true to say
that the majority of the population—farm servants, labourers and
factory operatives—were better off in terms of physical conditions
and aspirations for self-improvement than their parents or grand-
parents had been. Although church and burgh records provide a
very mixed picture of schools and educational opportunities, with
heritors failing to fulfil their obligations to provide stipends for a
local schoolmaster or funds for the upkeep of a school, the overall
investment in education was much greater by the end of the
eighteenth century than ever before. Yet the penalty of being poor
or unsuccessful was still extreme, as illustrated by the brutal
treatment of vagrants and travelling folk or gipsies, 'those savage
animals which increasing population and order expel or exter-
minate', and of beggars, 'little less troublesome'. Church session
records, with accounts of poor money distribution, suggest that a
clear line was maintained between the deserving and undeserving
poor.

Successful farmers and merchants and to some extent clergy
(though ministers were often recruited from the lesser branches of

landed families), constituted a small but growing middle class. The prosperous tenant farmer—imitating the manners and customs of the aristocracy—was a new element in Galloway. His fine, substantial dwelling house and farm buildings were a great improvement on the traditional long farm range, with cattle occupying one end. These houses were usually built of clay with a thatched roof and a 'lumm' to carry off the smoke. The *Statistical Account* of Whithorn provides a useful picture, contrasting the conditions of sixty years before with those of 1795:

> In farmers houses there were no windows of glass. The light was admitted through openings on each side of the house, and that in the windward side was filled with straw in blowing weather . . . The modes of living and clothing were in proportion, and consisted of the poorest fare and coarsest apparel. Now they live as well as any in Great Britain of their rank. The men are clothed, sometimes with home-spun, but more commonly with Yorkshire narrows, cotton velvets and corderoys. The women appear in printed linens, cottons and muslins. Here I speak of men and women in the lowest ranks of life; servants, cottagers, and mechanics . . . Almost every house has a seven-day clock; and watches are near as common as breeches.

The towns remained essentially small, conservative, closed communities, with local government and overall control of business and commerce dominated by the local landed families. Wigtown and Stranraer town council minute books provide an excellent picture of eighteenth-century town life. There is evidence of rudimentary town planning, with councils closing unsuitable 'tann pits', imposing regulations about alterations to houses, and improving drainage, streets and bridges. In Stranraer there were complaints of people not cleaning dung heaps or turf stacks from the fronts of houses and thus stopping up gutters, and keeping too many pigs in their closes or gardens. Other entries concern meal rationing and selling, town customs on shipping and trade, and the establishment of new industries. The following extracts from the Stranraer records (1780–8) typify one council's interests:

> 3 November 1787 . . . Every Cart Load of Salmon sold within the shades of the Town House to pay one shilling over and above the Custom and to Clean the Shades when done . . .

> 11 April 1782 . . . for years past Strowling peoples etc have taken the liberty to sell and dispose of Every kind of Goods without Molesta-

tion to the Prejudice of the free Traders of this Burgh. The Magistrates and Council being convened . . . and agreed to put the Laws against unfree Traders into immediate Execution.

There were few checks and balances to counter the local power of the country gentry. Tenant farmers were dependent on their goodwill, and the towns were too small to be of much influence. The Church was hardly a force for 'democracy', but rather an oligarchy controlled by the landowners and forced by them to relax its inflexible system of social discipline. The ownership of land and the possession of political power was concentrated in a few great families, usually interrelated by marriage and conscious of their responsibilities and privileges. One reason for the 7th Earl of Galloway's unpopularity in Court circles—as a Lord of the Bedchamber to George III—was his Scottishness. At the same time the ideal in Galloway was the imitation of the English country gentleman's lifestyle. The local gentry would do the European tour, create houses and parks, have their family and individual portraits painted by such leading artists as Allan Ramsay and the miniaturist Alexander Reid of Kirkennan, and perhaps retain the services of a black slaveboy, a decorative and fashionable status symbol. It is interesting that Sandy, the hero shepherd of William Nicholson's 'The Country Lass' (1814), acquired favour as Betty's suitor only after he became the heir to a slave owner:

> He had an uncle, without weans,
> Lived lang amang the sugar canes . . .
> And aften would himsel' solace
> Within their greasy black embrace.
> It's a' in taste.

Nicholson's conclusion concerning Sandy's miscegenation suggests a degree of tolerance which perhaps might be related to the presence in Galloway of at least one or two manumitted slaves.

There was no sharp dichotomy between the possession of land and participation in business and commerce. The careers of Samuel, Alexander and Ramsey Hannay of Kirkdale are good examples of the cross-connections between the different worlds of Galloway, London and the West Indies. The ranks of the aristocracy were in turn open to men of wealth who invested the profits of trade in land: William McDowall, a West Indian planter, bought the Garthland estate in Wigtownshire in the 1760s; Admiral John Campbell, son of a local minister; Thomas Rainy of Borgue, who used his great wealth from Dominica plantations to endow Borgue Academy in 1802; and Samuel Douglas of Georgia and Jamaica, who provided a free school for Kirkmabreck and Penninghame. Douglas was able to indulge some of his whims, requiring pupils to attend foundation services on 1 January each year.

The whole quality of life in Galloway depended upon the actions of the landed aristocracy, who had a monopoly of political and economic power. One approach to understanding the way power was divided in the community is to examine the representation of the Galloway constituencies in the eighteenth-century House of Commons. Central to the whole picture is the fact that men rarely became MPs because of political opinions. The MP represented the regional dominance and prestige of a particular family, and at the same time a means of ensuring for dependents and friends a share of government patronage relating to appointments and contracts in the navy, army, post office, and customs and excise departments.

The House of Commons had 558 members, of whom forty-five came from Scotland, including thirty from county constituencies, with Ayr, Wigtown, Kirkcudbright and Dumfries each electing one member. The vote in county seats was restricted to owners of land held from the Crown rated at £35 sterling, which meant in effect men with fairly large holdings. Most Scottish counties had between 100–200 voters, Ayr being unusually large with 200 in 1788. In the same year, Dumfries had 50–70, Wigtown 52, and the Stewartry 150. In each county the voters' roll was compiled annually before each election, though contests often more resembled disputes, with appeals to the Court of Session and House of Lords over the roll. Significantly, one important means a landowner could use to control a seat was to transfer property to create fictitious votes. Very few actual elections took place; contests in Galloway constituencies were held in only half the national elections.

The Scottish burghs had fifteen members elected by a system of indirect voting. Apart from Edinburgh, the burghs were arranged in groups of four or five—New Galloway, Stranraer, Whithorn and Wigtown (four votes) as the Wigtown Burghs seat, and Annan, Dumfries, Kirkcudbright, Lochmaben and Sanquhar (five votes) as the Dumfries Burghs. Each burgh council appointed a delegate, and these, meeting at each burgh in turn as the presiding burgh, elected the MP. As some burghs were little more than villages, and as most burghs were dominated by a self perpetuating group of 20–30 men, susceptible to every possible form of bribery, the elections were even less democratic than county contests. Members of the great families were often themselves burgh councillors; for example, John Hamilton of Bargany, the Earl of Stair, and Major-General William Dalrymple were in turn Provosts of Stranraer 1780–9. In Wigtown Burghs, the Stranraer vote was controlled by the Dalrymple Earls of Stair, and New Galloway to a lesser degree by the Gordons of Kenmure. As the votes for Whithorn and Wigtown were held by the Stewart Earls of Galloway, they in effect controlled the seat whenever Whithorn or Wigtown were the presiding burghs, since the delegate of the presiding burgh had a casting vote in the case of a tie. The 1784 election was an exception in that Stair, by cornering the Whithorn vote, was able to defeat the Galloway nominee.

In the counties, Dumfries was virtually a pocket seat of the Dukes of Queensberry, only the Marquesses of Annandale and the Johnstones of Westerhall providing any opposition. In Wigtownshire the main interests were the Earls of Galloway and Stair, with lesser families, in particular the McDowalls and the Agnews, in power-sharing compromises constantly negotiated over the election of members. In the Stewartry, different interests included the Duke of Queensberry, the Earl of Selkirk, the Earl of Galloway, Murray of Broughton, Stewart of Castle Stewart, Gordon of Kenmure, Heron and Maxwell.

This analysis perhaps presents a simplified picture, in that although the control of seats by the great families—particularly the Earls of Galloway—seems to represent an almost total monopoly of power, nevertheless it was true that family prestige was not always enough to secure the election of a particular nominee. Although election contests were usually avoided because they were so expensive, regional magnates could not ride entirely roughshod over the views of lesser men; it was necessary to cajole voters to a degree, to show concern for their friends and to pay attention to local individual and family issues. In most cases the formation of a clearly winning combination of two or three family alliances led to the withdrawal of competitors in advance of the election date, or to technically illegal compacts being made, where two or three candidates—as in the Stewartry in 1780 and in 1784 —agreed to share the seat, each holding it for two years.

The Earls of Galloway, represented by MPs who were their brothers, sons, relatives by marriage, or members of minor branches of the family, were the most important interest in Galloway. General James Stewart, the second son of the 5th Earl, was MP for Wigtown Burghs 1734-41 and 1747-54, and for Wigtownshire 1741-7 and 1754-61; and his brother William Stewart was MP for Wigtown Burghs 1741-7, in the interest of the 5th Earl, who died in 1746, and of the 6th Earl (1694-1773). John Stewart of Castle Stewart was MP for Wigtownshire 1747-54, and James Murray of Broughton was MP for Wigtownshire 1762-8 and for the Stewartry 1768-74 in the interest of the 6th Earl.

The 7th Earl of Galloway (1736-1806) wielded an enormous amount of power with a degree of selfish arrogance and greed probably related to his problems in providing for his fourteen children; he was neither respected nor liked. As Lord Garlies he purchased for himself the English seat of Morpeth 1761-8, and obtained Ludgershall 1768-73 from the government in exchange for returning George Augustus Selwyn for Wigtown Burghs (Selwyn vacated the seat for another Treasury nominee, Chauncy Townsend, the first Englishman to represent a Scottish constituency at Westminster). The 7th Earl's popular and able brother, Admiral Keith Stewart, was MP for Wigtown Burghs in 1762 and for Wigtownshire 1768-84. His son and heir, George Stewart, Lord Garlies, later the 8th Earl (1768-1834) was provided with English seats as MP for Saltash 1790-5, Cockermouth 1805-6, and Haslemere 1806; General Sir William Stewart, his second son, was MP for Saltash 1795-6, for Wigtownshire 1796-1802 and 1812-16, and for Wigtown Burghs 1803-5; his fourth son, Montgomery Granville John Stewart, was MP for the Stewartry of Kirkcudbright 1803-12; and his brother-in-law, Henry Watkin Dashwood, was MP for Wigtown Burghs 1775-80. William Stewart of Castle Stewart was MP for Wigtown Burghs 1770-4 and for the Stewartry 1774-80, and his brother, Alexander, represented the Stewartry 1786-94. Peter Johnston represented the joint Murray-Galloway interest as MP for the Stewartry 1780-1 and 1782-6. It was all a good deal more complicated than this summary may

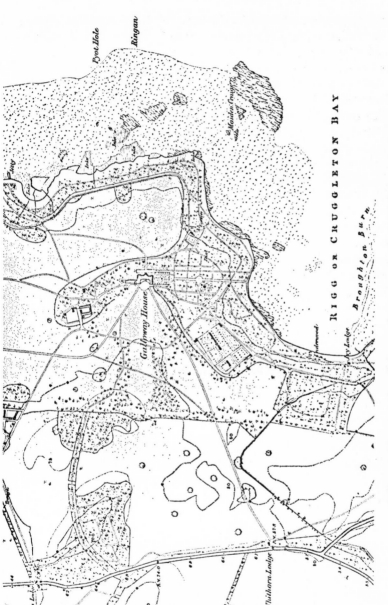

Galloway House and policies as shown on the first OS 6in map, 1850

suggest; Alexander Stewart, for example, unsuccessfully opposed the Galloway candidate, Peter Johnston, in 1780, and made a secret agreement with him and James Murray to divide up representation for the Stewartry in 1784.

By far the most interesting men in the Galloway family were Admiral Keith Stewart (1739–95) and General Sir William Stewart (1774–1827). Keith Stewart was perhaps not a very typical local MP. His long and successful naval career from the 1750s to the 1780s, with service in the West Indies, the Mediterranean and the North Sea, and his marriage to Georgina Isabella D'Aguilar, a member of a Portuguese Jewish family settled in England, gave him a wider tolerance than was usual in Galloway. He was at the same time an efficient improving landlord on his Glasserton estate, adding an unusual touch by bringing in farm labourers who had already learned new methods and techniques in England. Allan Ramsay's fine portrait (see plate on p 54), now at Cumloden, suggests something of his shrewdness and character. General Stewart served in the army in the Peninsular Wars in Spain and Portugal before retiring in 1814 to Cumloden. There his papers and letters include correspondence with his friend Admiral Horatio Nelson.

References for this chapter are on page 162

CHAPTER TEN

Life and labour, 1800–1900

The nineteenth century was a period of dramatic change in Galloway. Yet throughout the century the basis of its whole economy and way of life was the land. Industry, born essentially of the years of Industrial Revolution from 1780–1820, was largely land-based, utilising the primary products of agriculture and the major natural resource of water power. Such developments as tanning and leather-working, brewing, distilling, grain or meal milling and woodworking, which had been established in the years of industrialisation, continued on a modest scale in the towns and villages of the Province, though by mid-century some were going into decline. Other industrial activities expanded in the latter half of the century, especially woollen textiles and stone quarrying. There was, however, no set pattern, for as one textile trade declined, like cotton spinning in Gatehouse, another prospered, such as the tweed and blanket making of Kirkcowan and Newton Stewart. Similarly, metal mining (mainly lead ore) had mixed fortunes, while granite quarrying enjoyed a boom. Transport, too, was affected. With the extension of railway mileage and the building of branch lines to Kirkcudbright, Whithorn and Portpatrick, the small seaports of the Solway declined. The constant element throughout the century was thus farming, though it did not escape the vagaries of economic circumstance, involving necessary adaptation to new situations. Nevertheless Galloway remained an area of rural life with its very own characteristics.

For agriculture the 1800s were a period of contrasts, of booms and slumps, prosperity and depression. With its mixed farming economy, Galloway was perhaps less susceptible to depression than some of the great arable areas of southern England. Even during the relatively difficult period until the repeal of the Corn

Laws in 1846 Galloway remained an important cereal area, with a major export trade in grain through the Solway ports to surrounding urban, industrial districts, such as Lancashire and the west of Scotland. The pastoral farming, which today so typifies the area, began to reassert itself in the age of 'High Farming', 1845–75, assuming more of the significance it had in the days of the seventeenth- and eighteenth-century cattle-droving trade. As the improved communications of steamship and railroad opened up an international primary product market (in, for example, North American wheat and Argentinian beef), cereals became less important and farming moved towards more balanced production of arable crops, beef-fattening and dairying. The latter branch of farming expanded rapidly after the railway penetrated Galloway in the 1860s, putting most of the area within easy reach of urban markets. The reputation for fine milk products, particularly butter and cheese, was quickly established. The butter churn, cheese loft and presses were features of every farm of substance, and the cheese-making craft in both the Shire and Stewartry was highly regarded. According to the evidence gathered by the *Royal Commission on Agriculture* (1895), the rapid spread of dairying probably saved Galloway from the worst of the depression so badly felt elsewhere in Britain after 1875. The signs of the times were all too apparent: high rents and railway rates; high costs (for buildings, enclosure, drainage), and falling prices (due mainly to foreign competition). A number of co-operative cheese and butter factories had already been established and the Commission suggested that many more could be opened 'at comparatively small outlay'. By the end of the century there was a string of commercial dairies and creameries through Galloway, often built near the railway, and owned and operated either by private companies or by syndicates of local dairy farmers.

Something of the old way of life on the land survived into the early years of this century on farms and crofts in the more remote districts of the Moors, Machers and Glenkens. A glance at the first Ordnance Survey six-inch maps (compiled 1845–50) shows the beginnings of a long process of abandonment and rural depopulation from the marginal farming lands, which were given over to sheep or forest. The typical farmstead incorporated a primitive dwelling house, byre, cattle and sheep folds, built of rough rubble and slate, and perhaps a primitive corn kiln for drying grain prior to hand grinding by quernstones. Pulmaddy hamlet, on the Pulmaddy Burn about one mile upstream from its meeting with the Water of Ken about five miles north-west of Dalry, lay astride an ancient pack and drove route leading through the Glenkens from Carrick to the Stewartry. The settlement (see below), which incorporated at least four crofts, numerous corn kilns and a water-driven meal mill, was described as being 'in ruins' when visited by the Ordnance Survey engineers; it was probably abandoned sometime during the years of agricultural distress following the Napoleonic Wars. Many similar examples can still

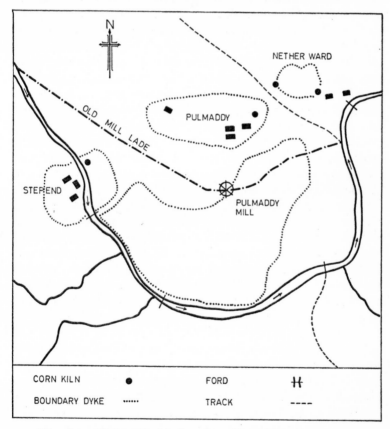

The site of Pulmaddy hamlet, 1850. Note the mill site, corn kilns, crofts, trackways and fords

be found, overgrown and ruinous, in the more remote districts of the Moors and Machers.

The landed estate was a major feature of nineteenth-century life and work in Galloway. Large parcels of the region were at that time concentrated in the hands of greater or lesser landowners, from the Stewarts of Shambellie, around New Abbey in the east, to the Agnews of Lochnaw in the Rhinns of Galloway. In between were landowners of consequence, like the modestly endowed Murrays of Cally and Gatehouse or the Earls of Stair, whose vast family patrimony totalled many thousands of acres. The life and work of a local community often revolved around such an estate, and an important historical source for this period is the extensive collection of family and estate papers assembled over the years by the Stairs and the stewards charged with the management of their lands. Here can be found an almost complete record of the day-to-day detail of estate supervision, farm leases, crop yields, tree plantations, ditching and dyking, as well as a vast archive of material relating to more general social and economic conditions. For example, local estate papers reveal that the McDowalls of Milldriggan Mill, Kirkinner, have worked there as millers for at least four generations. This sort of documentation, together with similar collections housed in the Scottish Record Office relating to the activities of the Murray, Hay of Park and Agnew estates, provides a valuable insight into the exploitation, with varying degrees of paternalism, of physical and human resources to maintain for the minority a lifestyle of relative ease. The Murrays of Cally, for example, by dint of careful estate management (see Chapters Six and Eight) laced with a mild paternalism, added to the amenity of their Georgian mansion, beautifying its pleasure grounds, entertaining house parties, and extending their influence in the political sphere through a parliamentary seat held by H. G. Murray-Stewart.

Yet for the majority, who were neither landowners nor town merchants, for the tenant farmers and their workforce, life on the land was hard and the rewards meagre even in times of relative prosperity. The following extract from the *Statistical Account* for Minnigaff parish (1842) gives a fair impression of the lot of the ordinary farm labourer and country craftsman of the period:

Farm servants, when boarded in the house, receive from L4,10s to

L6 the half-year. Married servants receive a certain quantity of meal, potatoes and money, in general from L18 to L20 a-year. The herds are allowed grazing and fodder for a cow and a calf, meal, potatoes, wool &c; and their income ranges from L16 to L24 yearly. The ordinary rates of wages for labourers is 1s to 1s6d a-day in summer, and 10d to 1s4d in winter. For cutting peats, 2s6d a-day is charged; and the same sum for mowing hay. When mowers of meadow hay are engaged for the season, they receive L2,5s to L2,10s and board. The season is generally about five weeks. Hay-workers, women or young lads, for the same period receive 18s to L1, and victuals. Female servants receive from L1,10s to L4 the half year.

Masons, who also work as slaters, charge 3s in summer and 2s6d in winter. Wrights charge 2s8d in summer and 2s6d in winter. Dike builders, 2s6d in summer, 2s in winter; in all without victuals. Dikes of dry stone cost from 1s4d to 1s8d per rood of 20ft long and 4½ft high, exclusive of carting of materials. For shoeing a pair of horses and keeping a plough in repair, L3 to L3,10s per annum. Shoeing a horse, 2s8d to 3s4d. An iron plough costs L4,10s to L5; a pair of harrows, L1,5s; a close-bodied cart, L8.

This certainly represented a substantial improvement in the social picture painted by earlier commentators like Robert Heron or the writers of parish entries in Sir John Sinclair's *Statistical Account* of the 1790s, but even in a rich agricultural area like Galloway poverty lingered amongst ordinary country folk. Rural under-employment and unemployment was omnipresent throughout the century; this reinforced the Church's traditional role as overseer of the poor, since apart from the landowner it was probably the most influential force in the community. Assessment was on the basis of real need, but was often inadequate: the poor of Girthon parish, a semi-industrial community incorporating part of Gate-house-of-Fleet, were paid in 1844 an average of 1s 4d weekly from the parochial aid fund. Even a wholly rural parish, like Dalry, had fifty poor, sharing the proceeds of assessment and kirk collections totalling just over £220. The scale and extent of poverty could still be exacerbated by natural vagaries, such as the failure of the potato crop through blight in the 1840s. A further complication was the growing influx of Irish poor, who were often not migrants or seasonal harvest workers as in the past, but more permanent settlers, particularly in Wigtownshire. Of the forty persons receiving aid in Stranraer, 'the bulk are natives of Ireland', wrote the Rev David Wilson in 1839, continuing his account by saying that 'having been brought up beggars, [they] have no disinclination to beg'.

The demise of rural industries and country crafts after the middle of the century caused further redundancy and social upheaval. Census and estate records give some idea of the scale, and reports of Parliamentary Commissions provide useful insights into working and living conditions in the mines, quarries and mills of south-west Scotland. Domestic textile craftsmen survived in some numbers, especially handloom weavers and fine workers, like the famous damask weavers of Sorbie parish. Parish entries in the (New) *Statistical Account* of the late 1830s and early 1840s give the impression of prosperity, but always (as the Rev Samuel Smith in his *General View of the Agriculture of Galloway*, published in 1810, was astute enough to realise) a reading between the lines gives a hint of impending disaster. The Gatehouse cotton mills are described in glowing terms, but already larger factories nearer urban markets were feeling the cold wind of competition from still bigger, more mechanised mills.

Agricultural change also had an impact on the social fabric of the Galloway countryside. As farms got bigger, especially in the thirty years of 'High Farming' after 1845, mechanisation appeared on the farm for the first time on any scale, and many agricultural labourers found themselves out of a job. The 1870s and 1880s brought difficult times for farmers, though in the words of John Spier in his report to the *Royal Commission on Agriculture in Scotland*, 'nothing like total collapse' existed in Galloway. He considered arrears of rent to be 'the best gauge of the condition of agriculture'; on one big estate in Wigtownshire these reached more than 20 per cent in 1887. In the years 1875–95 there were fifteen poor seasons and up to one-third of all farms in Wigtownshire changed hands. Many farmers were made bankrupt; their labourers, being redundant, were forced to seek new work or migrate from the land.

Although farming was the basis of life it also supported a wide range of country crafts, many of which were in their heyday in the nineteenth century. The joiner, carpenter, mason, smith, millwright, miller, weaver and tailor were to be found in every substantial village, serving the surrounding parish community. A typical parish occupational and social profile from the 1791 *Statistical Account* of Crossmichael in the Stewartry shows the

Page 107   Isle of Whithorn village and harbour. St Ninian's Chapel and a
promontory fort can be seen in the foreground

Page 108 (*Above*) Kirkandrews churchyard, clachan, shore and two-masted sloop c 1890; (*below*) Palnackie creek on the river Urr, seen at low tide. Ships of several hundred tons still use this little eighteenth-century harbour

sort of stratification which (the evidence of census data after 1841 seems to indicate) probably survived in most of Galloway until late in the nineteenth century:

Social Statistics of Crossmichael

Minister	1	Dyers	2
Schoolmaster	1	Shopkeepers	3
Steward-Depute	1	Innkeepers	2
Farmers (£15–170)	41	Male servants	51
Farmers (under £15)	27	Female „	54
Weavers	5	Millar	1
Shoemakers	4	Labouring cottagers	55
Tailors	7	Paupers	7
Blacksmiths	3		
Masons	10	Families	491
Joiners	6	Total Population	772

Here was a relatively prosperous community of lesser to middling farmers supporting upwards of forty craftsmen, whose day-to-day activities in workshop and on farm made Crossmichael almost entirely self-supporting. Similarly, Old Luce parish, which incorporated the turnpike roadside village of Glenluce and had a population of nearly 2,500 in 1841, was described as having 'no extensive manufactures', but nevertheless kept busy two corn and two (wool) carding mills, a dye and a flax mill.

The gradual rationalisation of farming and a measure of rural depopulation forced craftsmen to abandon the Galloway countryside and congregate in market towns like Castle Douglas or Newton Stewart or the larger villages like Kirkcowan and Glenluce. Many crafts merged: the carpenter and the joiner, the smith and the millwright. There was little mill building to be done by the end of the Victorian era and the machinery of farm threshing or meal mills was generally maintained by versatile country smiths of the stamp described in Ian Neill's *Country Blacksmith* (1966), which is set in the Machers of Wigtownshire. Some of the atmosphere of the old smithy and forge, where craftsmen turned their hands to every job from everyday horse-shoeing to the skilled making of chain harrows, can be captured in one of the few country blacksmiths' shops still working; at Mailzie near Kirkinner a water wheel works the simple tools that the smith needs to supplement his strong arm and anvil.

Life and labour, 1800–1900

By contrast to the host of declining crafts, such as millwrighting, brewing and tanning, a few old-established industries continued to flourish. Galloway had always been associated with various kinds of textile manufacture since the seventeenth century, and while those trades introduced during the Industrial Revolution—like cotton spinning and weaving, fine linen working (such as that of Sorbie) and muslin sewing—were on the decline by mid-century, the much older woollen industry was enjoying a substantially new lease of life. In Kirkcowan, Newtown Stewart, Creetown, Dalbeattie, New Abbey and Dumfries, blanket and woollen cloth weaving (especially the new 'tweeds' made fashionable by Sir Walter Scott) created employment for the skilled textile craftsmen of the south-west. Even in this forward-looking industry something of the old mode of production survived: Cumloden Waukmill, near Newton Stewart, with its internal water wheel to drive simple spinning and weaving machines and a modest group of workfolk, produced woollen blankets in the traditional way even in the early decades of the present century. Probably more typical were the larger Tarff and Wauk mills at Kirkcowan, the latter established on the banks of the Tarff Water by Robert Milroy in 1814. Milroy's two sons, William and Thomas, enlarged the mills in 1835. An official who was compiling the *Return of Factories* (1839) found thirty-nine employees hard at work tending looms driven by a 12hp water wheel. Waukmill was then described as 'a thriving establishment, manufacturing blankets, plain and pilot cloths, plaidings and flannels' mostly for export to traditional markets in industrial Lancashire and the west of Scotland. A later generation extended the factory still further, adding weaving sheds and installing steam power. The Milroys' original mill was a vast textile complex by the 1890s, probably the real hey-day of the Galloway wool trade. In common with so many others, large and small, the Wauk mill of Kirkcowan is now an interesting piece of industrial archaeology; no doubt it is a surprising site to anyone exploring the rural delights of Tarff Water valley.

The exploitation of woodlands and timber resources would not at first be readily associated with the textile industry, but a subtle link was to be found during the nineteenth century in another of Galloway's forgotten industries, pirn or bobbin making. This industry began on a small scale at the close of the eighteenth century, using wood and water-powered machinery to manufacture bobbins for local cotton and woollen spinning mills, like those at Gatehouse and Kirkcowan. There was a consequent and rapid growth of sawmills after 1800, and by about 1860 there were thirty-five in Galloway, mostly located on the larger estates and driven by water power. There are good examples at Logan Mills, near Ardwall, and in the grounds of Galloway House at Garlieston. The largest firm of bobbin makers was Thomas & William Helme of Dalbeattie, natives of Cumberland (another centre of bobbin manufacture) who settled in Galloway about 1840. Helmes soon had bobbin mills at Gatehouse (in the abandoned cotton mills) and Dalbeattie, as well as several woodyards and sawmills in the neighbourhood. Later the industry expanded considerably and until recently there were three firms producing a wide variety of bobbins for the textile trade.

Quarrying was another old-established Galloway industry which found new prosperity during the nineteenth century, thanks mainly to a succession of urban building booms. Apart from its use in general building, Galloway granite was much sought after for the construction of docks and harbours, for engineering and industrial use (bridges, stone rollers etc), as a facing stone in public buildings (often lending an air of stability to the façades of insurance offices or banks) and for city and town pavements. The main quarries were located around Dalbeattie (the 'capital' of the Galloway granite trade), on the edges of the Urr valley, and in the fells south of Creetown overlooking the Cree estuary. A prosperous export trade, at first by sea and later by rail, in all kinds of granite developed after the second decade of the century, the peaks of activity being the 1840s and 1890s. Heavily laden sloops carried off whole hillsides for use in the construction of the Thames Embankment and the Mersey docks, among other large schemes, and after the arrival of the railway the trade in crushed stone assumed a new significance. Stone polishing and the cutting of ornamental granite were soon established as related crafts, especially in Dalbeattie where there were a number of polishing mills. Although quarrying is still carried on, the scale of activity is modest, and the majority of quarries with their associated tramroads and harbours have long been abandoned to the industrial archaeologist.

The commercial interest of Galloway's larger towns—Castle

Douglas, Kirkcudbright, Newton Stewart and Stranraer—was alive to the opportunities presented by a large rural market of landowners, farmers and country folk. Castle Douglas early became the commercial heart of the Stewartry, while Stranraer and Newton Stewart vied for premier place in Wigtownshire, the former always being the front runner. Local trade directories and guide-books, like Gordon Fraser's *Wigtown and Whithorn* or William McIlwraith's *Visitors Guide to Wigtownshire*, show how extensive were the services provided by the local merchant community, in everything from haberdashery to the provision of a portable steam thresher at harvest time. In common with other rural areas, Galloway not only preserves a wide range of Georgian and Victorian period shopfronts, but also inside most shops some of the old world courtesy so rare in this age of supermarkets. Shops and shopping in one or more of the country towns of Galloway would make an absorbing local history project, particularly for an enthusiastic group of fifth or sixth formers.

For much of the century the internal trade of Galloway merchants, farmers, craftsmen and shopkeepers was carried along turnpike roads by horse and cart, but the external lifeline was the seaborne traffic of the Solway Firth. The extent of this sea-going activity can be seen in the numerous moribund ports and harbours on Solway shore, busy centres of trade and shipping during much of the nineteenth century (see Chapter Eleven). At modest Port William on the Luce Bay shore of the southern Machers or the more important Dalbeattie and its 'outport', Palnackie, in the estuary of the Urr, barks and luggers once tied up to load cargoes of farm produce for the markets of industrial Merseyside and Clydeside, discharging a vast range of domestic and other necessaries. After the 1860s the railway took over much of this trade; in the words of one commentator, 'it rendered the farmers an incalculable service [and] afforded them a quick and economical method of exporting their produce to centres of population and importing lime, tiles, implements and artificial manures'. The Wigtownshire Railway, which eventually linked Whithorn to Newton Stewart in 1877 and also had a branch from Millisle to Garlieston, had a considerable impact on the Machars district. Railway traffic figures for 1875–6, the first year of operations, are as follows:

Life and labour, 1800–1900

Wigtownshire Railway: Returns on Traffic Carried

1875	£	1876	£
April (7–30)	199	Jan	343
May	230	Feb	294
June	252	March	360
July	278	April	427
Aug (1)	527	May	516
Sept	475		
Oct	507		
Nov	441		
Dec	397		

Livestock and general merchandise made up the bulk of goods carried, although summer passenger traffic was of increasing importance. Undoubtedly the railway's second most significant contribution was the development of Galloway's considerable tourist potential, thus carrying on a traditional feature of the turnpike and coaching era.

It is perhaps appropriate to end this chapter by emphasising the unity and individuality of life in this remarkable corner of Scotland, features to a lesser or greater extent characteristic of Galloway at the present time. Historians looking at this dramatic century in retrospect tend to forget that there was no great discontinuity in the ordinary routine of the merchant or farm labourer. Although the Victorian era in particular brought radical changes to Galloway, the area still retained much of its essentially Georgian character—in, for example, its 'improved' agricultural landscape and planned villages. Yet beyond all doubt the old-world isolation of the Province was gone for ever, and by 1900 a growing national economy had almost entirely divested Galloway of the independence maintained in earlier centuries by regional self-sufficiency. Yet much of the documentary evidence and physical heritage of this past way of life remains, only awaiting discovery by the enthusiastic local, social or economic historian.

References for this chapter are on page 162

CHAPTER ELEVEN

Ports and harbours of Solway shore

Travelling to Galloway from the south, the visitor will probably drive up the M6 motorway before cutting west to Dumfries; coming from central Scotland he has an even shorter journey over trunk roads from Glasgow, Edinburgh or Ayr. These present-day roads follow the lines of old cattle-droving, military or turnpike routes, established during the eighteenth century. It is really only the visitor from Ireland who maintains the traditional mode of travel to and from Galloway—by sea. It is not difficult to imagine the significance of sea transport to this remote corner of south-west Scotland, isolated as it once was from the rest of the country by wild moor and mountain. Even in the age of the turnpike road and of the railway, the Solway Firth remained the economic lifeline of Galloway. Her trade in farm and other produce was largely carried across the Irish Sea to the industrial districts of Cumberland and Lancashire through the ports of Whitehaven and Liverpool, or by the Firth of Clyde to Glasgow and the west of Scotland. Imports of manufactures and other goods were brought to the Solway ports by the returning barks and luggers. Thus, during the eras of agrarian and industrial revolutions in the late eighteenth and early nineteenth centuries, numerous ports and harbours were developed by local merchants and landowners, and into these crowded the shipping so vital to the province.

Navigation in the Solway Firth is difficult everywhere because of dangerous sandbanks, violent currents and extreme tidal falls between high and low water. Nowhere is this more obvious than in the river Nith, where a 'bore' or tidal race, similar to that of the river Severn, can often be seen. Here treacherous sandbars and a constantly shifting channel posed major problems to shipmasters navigating its waters. Thomas Tucker, an English observer writ-

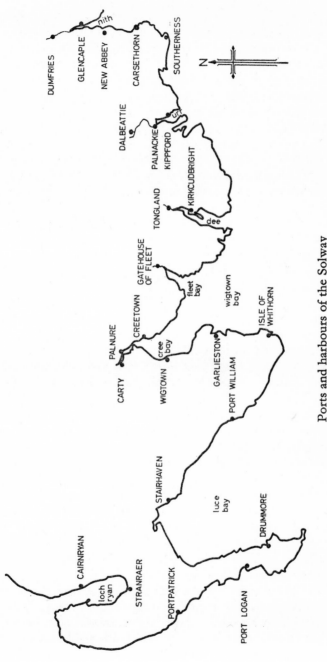

Ports and harbours of the Solway

ing in 1655, gave a fair impression of the effects these difficulties had on the town of Dumfries, for he said 'the badnesse of coming into the river [hinders] theyr commerce by sea'. Over the next two centuries the merchants and shipowners of the Nith battled against the elements to establish docks and harbours which would allow their ships and cargoes to tie up safely.

The first series of improvements began in the mid-eighteenth century, largely financed by the merchant burgesses of Dumfries. Two quays were built, one at Kingholm, a mile below the town, and the other at Glencaple in the parish of Caerlaverock nearer the mouth of the estuary. Both these old harbours preserve buildings of interest to the industrial archaeologist, including some fine Georgian domestic architecture, old warehouses and, at Kingholm, a group of early-nineteenth-century tweed mills. Glencaple is still used by the occasional coaster. Further down river and on the opposite shore are New Abbey Pow, probably a creek used since medieval times, and Carsethorn, the most southerly harbour on the Nith. At Carsethorn stands 'The Steam Packet Inn', and the remains of an old wooden jetty can be seen stretching out from the shore. Here are the only reminders of a regular steamship service to Whitehaven and Liverpool, which once linked all the ports of the upper Solway, including Port Carlisle and Annan. The only boats that tie up now are those used by the famous 'haff-net' fisherman of the Nith estuary who work this coast.

Southwards from Carsethorn lies Arbigland, the birthplace of Galloway's most famous sea-going son, Admiral John Paul Jones, founder of the United States Navy, who was born in an estate cottage in 1747. The dominating feature of the flat landscape in this parish of Kirkbean, however, is the lighthouse of Southerness, erected in 1749 by the merchants of Dumfries to guide shipping entering the Nith. Nearby is the old light mounted with a plaque, and the lighthouse itself—one of the finest examples of early navigational aids surviving in Scotland—is preserved as a monument to the long-vanished sailing ships which once navigated the treacherous waters offshore.

With the exception of the rocky and dangerous Portowarren and Portling—former haunts of smugglers, according to Joseph Train, the correspondent of Sir Walter Scott—there are no safe harbours until the estuary of the river Urr is reached. Quite apart from its historical interest this is one of the most outstanding scenic coasts in Galloway, closely rivalling that between Gatehouse and Creetown further to the west. The main channel of the Urr keeps close to Almorness Point and the Orchardton shore, before sweeping across Rough Firth to Kippford, an old centre of shipping and shipbuilding. Kippford (once known by the older name of the Scaur) was the main port of Colvend and Southwick and, in the late eighteenth century, ships set sail from here for the industrial areas of northern England and central Scotland with cargoes of barley, meal and potatoes. Another local export was millstones; according to the *Statistical Account* written in 1796, 'all the mills in south-western Scotland' were supplied from Colvend and 'some sent to Ireland'. Now one of the most popular yachting and sailing centres in the south-west, Kippford, with its picturesque setting, old inn and jetty, maintains at least some link with the days of the grander sailing ships built here before the turn of the century.

From Kippford the Urr twists and meanders northwards past abandoned granite quarries and old jetties to Palnackie (or Barlochan as it was once called), a small creek and harbour which was the centre of the Urr's seafaring community during the late eighteenth and nineteenth centuries. In the street leading to the harbour are some fine period dwellings and behind is the shell of an old corn mill. Like Glencaple on the Nith, the old port of Palnackie is still actively used by shipping and quite large coasters can often be seen high and dry on the mudflat alongside the quay, discharging cargoes of fertiliser or timber. Three miles upstream is the long-derelict port of Dalbeattie, known in the eighteenth century as Dub o'Hass. Robert Heron recorded in his *Observations* that at Dalbeattie 'mills and a small village seem to be thriving'. Certainly by the beginning of the nineteenth century Dalbeattie was an important centre of granite quarrying and general trade, with a merchant community actively involved in shipping and owning much of the sail that carried the produce of the fertile Urr valley to markets across the Solway. Today it is difficult to imagine a boat of any size navigating the tortuous meanders of the Urr as far as Dalbeattie.

Hestan Island (the Isle Rathan of S. R. Crockett's novel *The Raiders*, 1894), with its modern lighthouse and old copper mines, guards the entrance to Auchencairn Bay, which provided a sheltered but modest haven for shipping serving the parish of Rerrick. Further south on this rocky coast are the bays of Balcary, Rascarrel, Barlocco and Orroland, where boats beached at low tide would fetch and carry for local farming communities. Despite having no formal harbour, the extent of trade by sea from this Stewartry parish was considerable and probably typical of many coastal locations. The *Statistical Account* records the trade of Rerrick during 1794 as follows:

Imports	Exports
10,000 bushels of lime	15,280 stones of meal
General merchandise	800 bolls of barley
	230 bolls of bear
	198 bolls of wheat
	116 tons of potatoes

Further along the coast are Port Mary and Abbey Burnfoot, which have associations with the nearby ecclesiastical foundation of Dundrennan Abbey and the flight to England of Mary, Queen of Scots in 1568; neither can be described as harbours for they are little more than rocky inlets where boats may ride the waves in relative safety.

The port of Kirkcudbright on the river Dee is reached from the Solway by a narrow channel which winds its way from Torrs Point, past St Mary's Isle (the former home of the Earls of Selkirk, notable eighteenth-century improvers) to the dock at the river's edge above MacLellan's Castle. From the medieval period onwards Kirkcudbright was an important trading centre—though the famous eighteenth-century traveller, Daniel Defoe, writing in *A Tour through Great Britain*, published in 1727, clearly did not think much of it:

Here is a pleasant situation, and yet nothing pleasant to be seen. Here is a harbour without ships, a port without trade, a people without business: and that which is worse than all, they do not seem to desire business, much less do they understand it. They have a fine river, navigable for the greatest ships to the town quay. But alas, there is not a vessel that deserves the name of a ship belongs to it. In a word . . . they have a gold mine on their doorstep, and will not use it.

Later in the century, when agrarian change was proceeding apace, the visitor would have seen a place of industry and activity in what was by that time the largest port of Galloway, with a considerable domestic and foreign-going trade to the West Indies, the North American Colonies and the Baltic. The fine houses and shops built by local merchants and ship-masters in Castle Street and High Street are sufficient testimony of the town's prosperity at that time. Being an important centre of trade and shipping, Kirkcudbright was an obvious headquarters for the Customs and Excise Officers, ever vigilant for smugglers from France, Ireland or the Isle of Man running contraband ashore along the Solway. The harbour was formerly more extensive than the present-day breastwork; Victorian photographs show sailing ships berthed in the old dock, since filled in and now a car park. The modern harbour is unpretentious but busy; large numbers of fishing boats and coastal craft use the facilities and an oil tanker makes regular deliveries for the nearby storage depot.

Less than two miles north of Kirkcudbright, near Thomas Telford's Tongland Bridge, is the ultimate limit of navigation on the river Dee, where until the latter half of the nineteenth century small barks tied up to land cargoes of lime and general merchandise for delivery to surrounding inland parishes. It was here 'at the tideway of the River Dee' that the Glenkens Canal was to begin, an improbable scheme to carry navigation as far as the head of Loch Ken near Dalry. Joseph Priestly describes the whole project in his *Historical Account of the Navigable Rivers, Canals and Railways throughout Great Britain*, published in 1831. A number of landed gentry and businessmen, including Sir William Douglas (see Chapter Eight), were associated with the scheme. According to the *Statistical Account* for Tongland parish for 1793, exports from the Dee salmon fisheries, below the once famous falls which the projected canal was intended to bypass, reached markets in Liverpool, Manchester and even London.

Skirting Kirkcudbright Bay and Little Ross the coastline sweeps north-westwards. Three large bays on this shore, Ross, Brighouse and Kirkandrews, provided shelter for small barks serving the farms of Borgue and Girthon. Offshore in Wigtown Bay are the Islands of Fleet, guarding the entrance to Fleet Bay at the head of which stands Gatehouse. Today the straight course of the Water of Fleet between Ardwall and Boatgreen marks the line of the long-abandoned canal to Port Macadam, just upriver from Cardoness Castle. This old canal was built at the beginning of the nineteenth century to improve access to the planned, industrial village of Gatehouse; Alexander Murray of Broughton and Cally, son of James Murray, the founder of the village, was responsible for initiating the project. Gatehouse had a large sea-going trade, mostly generated by the industries and crafts developed in the village during the Industrial Revolution (see Chapters Six and Eight).

The coast road between Gatehouse and Creetown commands a superb panorama of Wigtown Bay and the Cree estuary with the shore of the Machers in the distance. Several rocky coves are associated with local smuggling legends—particularly Dirk Hatterick's Cave and Kirkdale Port—but the first man-made harbour on this side of the estuary is below the Kirkmabreck granite quarries. From the second decade of the nineteenth century onwards whole hillsides of granite were transported by sea from the two quays here to the Mersey in ships of the Liverpool Dock Trustees, and vast footages of granite were supplied to other cities to provide building stone or pavement for urban street improvement. Creetown (formerly known as Ferrytown of Cree), another interesting former industrial and seafaring village with a small tidal harbour, is itself almost entirely built of Kirkmabreck granite. Further north toward Newton Stewart is the creek of Palnure, once a shipping point for the lead mines of Blackcraig and Machermore, which were worked by various English and Scottish partnerships during the era of widespread metal mining in the late eighteenth and early nineteenth centuries. According to the second *Statistical Account* for Minnigaff parish dated 1842, vessels of up to 60 tons could reach the 'small quay at Palnure Bridge' to discharge cargoes of coal, lime, bone-meal and slate, and carry out grain, potatoes, timber and bark (probably for leather tanning). Looking at these mud-flats today it is difficult to imagine.

On the opposite shore of the estuary just above this point is the highest creek on the Cree, called Carty Port, and nearby is one of the few country brick and tile works still active in the south-west. The present New Quay in St Ninian's Creek, long deserted, was constructed by the Earl of Galloway in the early nineteenth century, and replaced an even earlier one upstream. Kelly Port, a mile or so downriver, is even more derelict, though the remains of the old jetty there can still be traced. Between Kelly Port and Wigtown there are several points on the shore of the Moss of

Cree, notably Knockdown and Barsalloch, where ferries plying from the Kirkmabreck shore used to land their passengers.

Wigtown, at the mouth of the river Bladnoch, has had a harbour since the medieval period, the first being located north of the castle, immediately below the kirk. Thomas Tucker reported in 1655 that 'there comes sometimes a small boate from England with salt or coales', while Andrew Symson in his *Large Description of Galloway* said Wigtown had 'little trading by sea'. During the latter half of the eighteenth century, navigation was improved and the harbour was busy with ships loading the farm products of the neighbourhood for export to the Clyde and Mersey. The customs port of Wigtown included every creek from the Mull of Galloway to the mouth of the river Dee. The course of the Bladnoch was diverted into a more southerly channel in 1817 by the erection of breakwaters and a new harbour built by the burgh council. Steamers made their appearance in 1825 and a regular service to Whitehaven and Liverpool was established soon after. As late as 1877 a local commentator could write that 'the railway has not yet superseded the harbour, for a mast or two denote the presence of a sloop or schooner', and the steamboat *Countess of Galloway* still provided a twice-monthly service to Liverpool. But the coastal trade soon collapsed once the railway became established. The description of Wigtown harbour by the Rev C. H. Dick in his *Highways & Byways* is still appropriate today, for he found it 'occupied by one small rowing boat'.

Beyond Baldoon Sands and Orchardton Bay are Brandy Port (the name speaks for itself in this smuggling country) and Innerwell with its fishery. Further south round Eggerness Point in a fine, sheltered bay is Garlieston, the major harbour of the southern Machers. Garlieston is a fine example of a Georgian seafaring village, laid out on a crescent plan at the end of the eighteenth century (see Chapter Six). Its harbour has been rebuilt several times since and when a branch of the Wigtownshire Railway reached the village in 1876 a tramway extension to it was opened from the station. Garlieston was an important staging point for the Solway steamers plying to Liverpool during the nineteenth century and as late as the early decades of this century summer excursion steamers sailed to Douglas, Isle of Man. Today the port is used by a modest group of inshore fishing boats. There is much to interest the industrial archaeologist here, including old warehouses and granaries, the derelict railway line and station, and in the policies of Galloway House an abandoned sawmill with a cast-iron water wheel.

Isle of Whithorn has a more ancient harbour dating back to the days of James IV of Scotland, under whose authority it was built. Bishop Pococke in his *Tours in Scotland* describes Whithorn in 1760 as 'a little harbour formed by a pier' into which ships of 300 tons might enter. Its trade at that time was mainly in the export of barley and other produce and the import of lime for land improvement. The pier was extended with the aid of the Convention of Royal Burghs in 1790 and further improved at later dates. The harbour is difficult of access due to tidal races and rocks, and the pier has had to be rebuilt several times following storm damage. On the landward side of the harbour are a range of former grain stores and warehouses, the Steam Packet Inn—with a painting of the steamer *Countess of Galloway* above the door, and a fine period Custom House. The harbour today is busy with pleasure craft and the occasional fishing boat.

There are only two harbours of any consequence along the whole eastern shore of Luce Bay: one at the little village of Port William in the parish of Mochrum and the other at Stairhaven, a few miles south of Glenluce. The coast is intermittently rocky with farmsteads perched on the raised beach or cliff-lined with few inlets likely to serve as harbours, the possible exception being the pebble foreshore at Changue, Chippermore, Corwall and Garheugh, where sloops once beached. Port William was described in 1796 as 'a small neat village' with a busy harbour and mill. Prior to this it had been a centre of salt panning, an industry which developed on a larger scale on the opposite shore of Luce Bay. The harbour, with its old dockside buildings, has probably changed little, though an increasing number of pleasure craft and sea-angling boats are now based here. By contrast the former pier at Stairhaven is a depressing sight, only the landward end remaining. The Bay of Kirkchrist, in which Stairhaven—or the Crow's Nest as it was formerly known—is situated, was one of three beaching places serving Old Luce parish at the end of the eighteenth century, and the jetty here was built by the Earl of Stair after whom it is named.

Luce Sands stretch from the mouth of the Water of Luce to the pleasant seaside village of Sandhead, but from Ardwell Mill southwards the shoreline narrows past Dyemill (an old wool mill), Chapel Rossan (the site of an old salt works), Logan (where there is a well-preserved windmill tower) and Terally to reach Drummore, the most southerly harbour in Scotland. Drummore was built in the eighteenth century to facilitate the trade of its immediate hinterland, the farming country of Kirkmaiden parish. A plan dated 1864 in the Stair Papers at the Scottish Record Office shows the 300ft-long quay with a dredged sandbar to landward, providing good shelter from southerly winds.

In common with the upper Solway, the Irish Sea coast of the Rhinns has many bays where small sailing ships could beach at low tide in favourable weather, yet there are only two natural harbours on this treacherous coast. They share a common and tragic history. Port Logan and Portpatrick were at the centre of a national controversy over the short-sea passage to Ireland, which raged for more than a century after the 1760s. The government's main concern was fast communication with Ireland for both mails and troops; the problem was to decide on the quickest and most reliable route across the 20-mile-wide North Channel. Many different routes had been followed before the eighteenth century, though the established one for mail packets was from Portpatrick to Donaghadee. The hazards to navigation, especially unfavourable winds and currents, caused interminable delays in passage, and soon merchant and landed interests on either side of the Irish Sea joined the political lobby for a government inquiry into communication between Scotland and Ireland.

The first of many commissions, led by a veritable cortège of eminent engineers, reported in 1768, when John Smeaton found Portpatrick 'almost in a state of nature', except for a small landing place for travellers. He proposed two outer breakwaters to guard the rocky entrance and the reconstruction of the inner harbour. Work was completed ten years later, having cost twice the original estimate. After further misadventures the government appointed Thomas Telford to carry out another investigation. After his visit to Portpatrick in 1802 Telford reported that the site 'was destitute of the advantages requisite for a perfect Harbour for packets to ply from', where winds from every direction except the east caused a heavy swell and 'large reefs of rocks' made entry to the harbour hazardous on any but calm days. The Telford survey thus produced no definite conclusions, but another outstanding civil engineer, John Rennie, supported the further development of the Portpatrick–Donaghadee crossing and the improvement of the harbour at Portpatrick by the construction of two massive piers and a lighthouse. Work went ahead slowly after 1820, but sixteen years later only the South Pier with its 46ft-high lighthouse was complete, while the North Pier remained unfinished. A severe storm in 1839 caused further setbacks. Opposition to the route continued to mount from all sides and a Post Office report of 1836 was highly critical of the expenditure at Portpatrick. The Irish mails were diverted to the Stranraer–Larne route in 1849 and, despite the efforts of the railway companies to revive the short-sea crossing, by 1873 Portpatrick was all but abandoned and the harbour works left to the ravages of the sea.

Some ten miles south of Portpatrick is Port Logan (or Nessock), which has a similar if less dramatic history. As early as 1715, John Adair, a cartographer and 'Geographer for the Kingdom of Scotland', carried out a survey of the west coast of Galloway and reported that he 'did not see a fit and convenient place for making a harbour to shelter ships, packet boats and other vessels, except the corner of the Bay of Nessock, which by building a good pier or head, they can lie safe and secure in all weather'. The present pier (now badly ruined), lighthouse, sea-wall and houses were built during the second decade of the nineteenth century by Colonel Andrew McDowall, whose main interest was in the developing Irish cattle trade. Thomas Telford is believed to have designed Port Logan, now a crumbling little pier in a forgotten corner of Galloway.

Portpatrick's strongest rival in the controversy over the North Channel crossing was Stranraer at the head of the comparatively sheltered Loch Ryan. Before the beginning of the nineteenth century the harbour there was of little consequence, its only major trade, like that of Cairnryan on the opposite shore, being in imported Irish cattle and the export of local farm produce. After the 1840s, however, Stranraer quickly became established as the premier Scottish port on the Irish crossing. This status was afterwards confirmed when the railway companies and the Post Office recognised it as the official packet station in preference to Portpatrick. The old harbour still survives but the seafront is dominated by the East Pier, built and extended after 1863 and now the focus of all cross-channel traffic.

Page 125 Relics of rural life and industry: (*above*) Crossmichael mill, near Castle Douglas; (*below*) Galloway House estate sawmill

Page 126 (Above) The Square, Auchencairn c 1906, showing summer visitors on a scenic drive; (below) a Dumfries-bound mixed passenger and goods train steams into Castle Douglas station in Glasgow & South Western Railway days c 1910

Ports and harbours of Solway shore

The shores of Galloway are dotted with fascinating and often long-abandoned creeks and harbours. Others have been more fortunate, surviving as modest fishing ports or centres for yachts and pleasure craft. Only a few like Kirkcudbright or Stranraer are actively used by vessels of any great tonnage. All the old harbours have a history of their own, generally one of service to an isolated farming community in an age of sailing sloops, and all but a few survive as they were abandoned, retaining much of interest to the industrial archaeologist or the casual visitor.

References for this chapter are on page 162–3

CHAPTER TWELVE

Victorian and Edwardian tourists

The turnpike road and the stage coach made all but the most remote parts of the country accessible to travellers and brought about the first wave of tourism in Britain. This phase lasted until the middle of the nineteenth century when the railway ushered in a new era of mass communications and even the poorest could afford to travel at the rate of a penny a mile.

Countless tourist guides and gazetteers, produced in the first decades of the nineteenth century, show how comprehensive were the coach routes and how excellent the communications provided by the turnpike roads. These guides are full of detailed information about the locality, points of interest and antiquity, scenic viewpoints and the accommodation and facilities available in the coaching inns along the way. Two such guide books, published in 1827—*The Scottish Tourist* (Stirling and Kenney, Edinburgh), 'respectfully dedicated to Sir Walter Scott, Bart, of Abbotsford', and Robert Chambers' *Picture of Scotland* (William Tate, Edinburgh)—had their precursors in the 'tours' of Daniel Defoe and Robert Heron (see Chapter Seven). Heron's *Observations* was widely read and ran into several editions, while *The Scottish Tourist* would have been the constant travelling companion of the well-organised coaching party.

The main turnpike route through Galloway followed roughly the present-day A75 Dumfries–Portpatrick road; along its way were tollhouses, change houses and coaching inns. After the 1820s, steamships were a familiar sight in the Solway ports; these provided links with Glasgow and Liverpool and attracted a very considerable passenger traffic to Galloway. The typical visitor would most likely start his trip at Dumfries and afterwards, like Robert Heron, follow the turnpike road westward, staying at coaching inns in the main towns en route—Castle Douglas, Kirkcudbright,

Victorian and Edwardian tourists

Gatehouse-of-Fleet and Newton Stewart—in order to explore more readily, on horseback or by horse and carriage, the coast and historic sites. The watering places, like Southerness, Rockcliffe or Portpatrick, were very likely to attract the Georgian or early Victorian tourist, who might rent a house or lodge in some respectable establishment for the season. Among the visitors early in this period was Robert Burns, combining business with pleasure, as he always did with such remarkable facility, during his regular stays at Kirkcudbright and Gatehouse. Thomas Carlyle, a native of Dumfries-shire, did much to attract his readers to Galloway, writing that 'there is no finer or more beautiful drive in the Kingdom than the one round the shore of the Stewartry, by Gatehouse of Fleet'.

The development of a more formal tourist trade in the latter half of the nineteenth century can be ascribed to three main causes. First, and perhaps most critical, there was the penetration of Galloway's landward fastness by the railway, which for the first time afforded speedy communication with most of Britain and put the area within a comfortable half-day's journey of central Scotland and much of the north of England. In 1859 the Castle Douglas and Dumfries line from the Glasgow & South-Western Railway in Nithsdale was completed and the whole Galloway line to Portpatrick opened two years later. Several important branch lines were built, notably from Castle Douglas to Kirkcudbright (1864) and from the main line to Stranraer harbour (1863). The Wigtownshire Railway, a largely locally promoted scheme to provide the Machers district with better communications, was finally opened to Whithorn in 1877. The last important link to the railway network of central Scotland (principally those of the Caledonian and G & SW Railways) was established when the Girvan and Portpatrick line was opened to traffic the same year. Certainly by the early 1860s much of Galloway became accessible to growing numbers of railway travellers, tourists, holidaymakers and commercial gentlemen. Soon new hotels were being opened and old coaching inns refurbished in mid-Victorian style to cater for this expanding trade.

The second, yet undoubtedly less tangible, cause was the influence of Victorian romanticism on the middle and upper class, best seen in the cult of medievalism and the Gothic revival in literature, art and architecture. Added to this was the popular awareness of history; the mass reading public had an apparently insatiable appetite for the Victorian novel. Much of this was due to the works of Sir Walter Scott, especially the Waverley Novels, with their evocation of the romantic and mysterious in Scottish history. Scott drew heavily on the heritage and history of south-west Scotland, largely through the influence of his assiduous correspondent there, Joseph Train. One of his best early historical novels, *Guy Mannering* (1815), is partly set in Galloway, and in others, such as *Old Mortality* and *The Antiquary* (both 1816), Scott made advantageous use of local historical legends, events and personalities. Victorian tourists, inspired by Scott's romantic view of Scottish history, came in search of the actual settings and scenery—the abbeys (like Dundrennan and Sweetheart), the castles and tower houses (like Caerlaverock and Threave), and the sea coasts and caves of the smugglers and raiders.

Later nineteenth-century novelists, particularly those of the 'Kailyard School' (a 'group' of Scottish writers who rejected realism for the romantic), followed doggedly in Scott's footsteps, the most commercially successful being Samuel Rutherford Crockett, himself a Gallovidian. His first major novel, *The Raiders* (1893), evoked Galloway's remote and mysterious character, and this was exploited in many of his later books, some of which were excrutiatingly bad. More to Crockett's credit were his popular guide books, the best being *Raiderland; or all about Galloway* (1904). In short, the literature of Galloway, especially the widely popular novels of Scott and Crockett, did much to bring the romantic and historical associations of the area to the attention of a wide audience of prospective visitors.

Lastly—a factor common to Victorian Britain as a whole—was the recovery of landed society in the mid-nineteenth century and, associated with this, the rise of country houses and revival of older ones. The escape of Queen Victoria and the royal family to country estates like Osborne, Sandringham and Balmoral set a trend assiduously followed by the urban *nouveaux riches*, often second-generation industrialists and businessmen able to take life easy at a time when Britain was truly the 'workshop of the world'. At the same time the older established landed gentry benefited from the general prosperity of the later Victorian years (particularly in farming until the mid-1870s) and were able to revitalise their family patrimonies by the extension and development of estates. Galloway has many examples of mansions in Scottish baronial style, often built by businessmen from the north of England or central Scotland for summer holidays or retirement. Understandably the fashion for regular escape from the urban, industrial environment filtered down to the middle classes, who were soon taking their vacations in the scenic and romantic countryside so easily reached by rail.

Galloway, like the Lake District, was in an ideal situation to exploit the tourist traffic of the new railway age. Yet, for a variety of reasons, it was less successful than its counterpart across the Solway Firth and never attained the widespread popularity of, for example, the west Highlands or Snowdonia. Nevertheless its wide range of attractions brought many thousands of Victorian tourists to Galloway year after year. The hills and moors, rivers and lochs, cliffs and bays, combined with peace and quiet and romantic or historical associations, provided an environment ideally suited to the escapist. The romantic Victorian was especially attracted by dark, forbidding lochs, mysterious, ruined castles and tumbling streams and waterfalls. Glen Trool and the Grey Mare's Tail, for example, were recommended in the pages of every guide book published since the late eighteenth century; generations of visitors went there on foot, on horseback, by pony and trap or stylish Edwardian motor-car.

Despite dangerous tides and limited stretches of good sand, the sea coasts of the Solway, Luce Bay and the Rhinns of Galloway have always attracted the holidaymaker. Even in the late eighteenth century Southerness was a popular place for sea-bathing and in the coaching age substantial number of tourists came to take the air on their visits to the coast from Southerness in the east to Portpatrick in the west. Later in the nineteenth century Southerness, Sandyhills, Rockcliffe, Kippford, Balcary, Isle of Whithorn, Monreith, Sandhead and Portpatrick became holiday resorts, while numerous other sandy shores were within easy reach by pony and trap from the main railway towns of Dalbeattie, Newton Stewart and Stranraer. Portpatrick became established as the main seaside resort in the south-west not just because of its obvious popularity but as the direct result of the publicity showered upon it by the railway companies.

Spas were popular with the upper and middle classes throughout much of the nineteenth century, and Galloway had several

modest wells where the waters might be taken. One of the most
celebrated of these was at Lockenbreck near Laurieston, where
until the turn of the present century it was possible to be accommodated in a small hydropathic hotel and drink the local waters at
Lochenbreck Well. 'The spring is copious', writes Robert
Chambers in his *Picture of Scotland*, 'the water transparent and by
no means unpleasant to the taste.'

Characteristic of the Victorian age was the enthusiasm for the
past—partly inspired by the widespread popularity of historical
novels such as those of Sir Walter Scott. Dilettante antiquarians
and archaeologists came to Galloway to draw, paint and later to
photograph tower houses, castles and abbeys. No self-respecting
antiquary could overlook the historical attractions of an area like
that around Whithorn, where the tour would include the Priory,
St Ninian's Chapel at Isle of Whithorn and St Ninian's Cave on
Glasserton shore. The more assiduous tried their hand at a bit of
amateur archaeology—sometimes with care and success, more
often with wreckless abandon. The majority of travellers, however, took an intelligent interest in the local history, confining
their enthusiasm to what could be seen above ground—in the fine
remains of Sweetheart, Dundrennan and Glenluce abbeys, and the
awe-inspiring fortresses of Threave or Cardoness.

The sportsmen were even more active, eager to try their luck
with rod or gun. At one end of the scale was the shooting or
fishing party accommodated at the big house or at a lodge on the
moors, usually as guests of the landowner. Gavin Maxwell, in his
autobiographical book *The House of Elrig*, describes the lavish
entertainment of such house parties in his father's family in the
early years of this century. The other extreme was represented by
the residents of a local hotel or inn with fishing rights on a stretch
of river or moorland loch. Then, as now, fishing was the major
attraction for the sportsman in Galloway.

The wild and romantic hills were a magnet for ramblers and
hill walkers who came to Galloway in increasing numbers following its penetration by the railway. Probably the most popular
areas for hill walking were Glen Trool, Merrick and the Rhinns of
Kells, though those around Criffell and the hills above Gatehouse
also attracted many walkers. Guide books devoted considerable
space to the outstanding opportunities for hill and coastal walking
which the region presented. The first to be written specifically

with the walker in mind was Malcolm Harper's *Rambles in Galloway* (published in 1876), while C. H. Dick's *Highways and Byways in Galloway & Carrick* was the end-product of many years spent cycling through the Galloway countryside.

Galloway has a long-standing reputation among visiting artists, who are attracted by the clarity of light and definition of landscape. Local artists, too, contributed to the image of Galloway as an artists' haven. Among them were the brothers John and Thomas Faed of Barlay Mill, Gatehouse-of-Fleet, who produced portraits, landscapes—drawn largely from Galloway scenery, and innumerable 'romantic' pieces inspired by such Scottish ballads as the 'Mitherless Bairn' and 'The Cotter's Saturday Night'. Such was Victorian taste, for both became members of the Royal Academy of Arts. If native artists were influential in drawing the scenic and romantic attractions of Galloway to the attention of the middle classes, those artists who came to live and work in the area were more influenced by the international art scene; they in turn brought to the area, and to Kirkcudbright in particular, something of the flavour of impressionism and *art nouveau*. Outstanding in this respect were members of the 'Glasgow School' of artists and above all E. A. Hornel, some of whose work may be seen in Broughton House, his former home in Kirkcudbright's old High Street.

The biggest expansion of the tourist trade took place after 1875, by which time most of Galloway could be reached by rail. This quickly led to a development of new hotels to cater for its needs —notably those built by the railway companies at either end of Galloway in Portpatrick and Dumfries. The railway also brought increasing numbers of family holidaymakers as well as a developing day-trip trade, with special excursions being run from Glasgow, Edinburgh, Carlisle and Dumfries to places like Portpatrick and Whithorn. Today's railway and steamship enthusiasts would have been fascinated by one excursion—by steamer from Garlieston (terminus of the Wigtownshire Railway) to Douglas, Isle of Man—run by the railway companies in association with the Isle of Man Steam Packet Company.

There was a remarkable range of literature on Galloway from which the nineteenth-century visitor might make his choice. The Georgian tourist companions were followed by numerous more detailed local guide books, published at intervals throughout the

Advertisement from *Rambles Round Creetown and District*, 1912

latter half of the nineteenth century. Two standard works were Maxwell's *Guide to the Stewartry of Kirkcudbright* (Castle Douglas, 1878, and many subsequent editions) and W. McIlwraith's *Visitors Guide to Wigtownshire* (Stranraer, 1875). One of the most informative guides to a particular locality of this period is *Wigtown and Whithorn: historical and descriptive Sketches* (Wigtown, 1877) by Gordon Fraser, a local stationer and printer. Fraser had an eye for detail which makes his book as invaluable a source for

Victorian and Edwardian tourists

the historian as it must have proved to the Victorian tourist. One cannot praise too highly the outstanding guide by the Rev C. H. Dick; first published by Macmillan in 1916, *Highways and Byways* has recently and most deservedly been reprinted and should have pride of place on the bookshelf of every lover of Galloway. It captures all the atmosphere of the Edwardian era—an age of bicycles on dusty roads—and the timeless quality is well caught by Dick's own 'watch-the-birdie' tripod camera.

It is perhaps appropriate to end this chapter in the Edwardian twilight of C. H. Dick's cycle trips over Galloway byways. Probably more visitors came to the region in that heyday of railway travel at the beginning of this century than at any time until the present age of mass car ownership. In attracting individual types of visitor or holidaymaker, Galloway differed radically from the Lake District or the Firth of Clyde, which were always much more accessible to the wider public from such centres as Manchester and Glasgow. Today tourists of every kind come to Galloway, yet they look for the same magical qualities which attracted the middle-class Victorians—peace and quiet in a sympathetic environment where heritage and natural scenery still combine in a relatively unspoiled region of Britain.

References for this chapter are on page 163

CHAPTER THIRTEEN

Churchyards and memorials

The commemorative tombstones found in many Galloway churchyards are probably the best surviving examples of local vernacular art and very well worth preserving and studying for their own sake. The churchyards themselves—usually beside the parish churches—are rarely vandalised and appear well cared for but at the same time lacking the clinical uniformity of modern burial grounds. Parish churches, though part of the Presbyterian Church of Scotland, were often built on the site or beside the remains of pre-Reformation churches or foundations. Many date from the late eighteenth and early nineteenth centuries, during a period of rapid increase in the rural population, and are simple, well-proportioned structures following classical form, with later Victorian spires and additions.

The practice of erecting upright or table stones as memorials only became fashionable in Galloway in the later seventeenth century; the most interesting of these, mainly commissioned by landowners, farmers, merchants and skilled artisans, date from c 1700–1850, the best examples belonging to the second half of the eighteenth century. Although today some churchyards tend to be invested with a Gothic atmosphere of chill and even distraught melancholy, the eighteenth-century stones reflect an attitude of quiet acceptance appropriate to a period of high mortality. Death at that time was not only a good deal less anonymous but was encountered more frequently and at different stages of the life cycle than is usual today. During a man's lifetime his brothers, sisters, parents, children, wife or wives, and even grandchildren might die, and one way of keeping their memory alive was to erect personal monuments in stone.

The churchyards included in the list on pages 138–145—which is not intended to be comprehensive—are the most important in terms of the technical detail of the sculpture and epitaphs of their memorial stones and also in terms of the overall atmosphere. For genealogists, the stones provide confirmatory evidence of general social trends, such as the heavy infant and child mortality rate, the incidence of cholera and the dangers of sea travel resulting from the disasters and wrecks in British coastal waters that are recorded there; they also supply some indication of local customs—for example, on a Scottish gravestone the death of a wife will be inscribed under her own maiden name, just as in legal documents where the name of a married woman occurs the maiden name is also given. The main importance of the memorials, however, is the visual record of the skilled, painstaking and specialised workmanship of Galloway stone masons in the preparation and use of local stone, the cutting of lettering and the creation of lively, imaginative and original sculptures. Some of the stones in neighbouring churchyards seem stylistically to be the work of particular craftsmen or their pupils—for example, the Girthon–Anwoth–Kirkcudbright group, but little is known about the masons involved. Though they may remain anonymous, their work stands up amazingly well to assessment today, even if that of the versifiers does not. The epitaphs do, however, include some grand reading matter, occasionally of hilarious vulgarity.

The symbols on the stones are of two types. The first are directly concerned with death and with Biblical references: cherubs, sometimes angelic, sometimes fearsome, representing the soul of the departed; angel wings, usually sprouting from near the ears, symbolising the hope or belief that the soul was on its way to Heaven; skulls, cross-bones, coffins, spades, and skeletons, symbols of death; winged or plain hour-glass, the passage of time; scales of justice, the Last Judgement; with the Tree of Knowledge, the serpent, and Adam and Eve from the Creation story in the *Book of Genesis*; and the Bible, often with text specified, providing an appropriate commentary. The second group of symbols are basically impedimenta representing the occupation and status of the person or persons commemorated—such as a plough team for a farmer; a spade, rake and hoe for an estate gardener, or other suitable items for masons, smiths, or gamekeepers—and, less commonly, visual representations of a family group or weeping children mourning the loss of children or parents.

The Covenanting memorials in churchyards and on hillsides

form a special class; ostensibly monuments to honour the dead, they are in reality primarily the product of fanaticism and religious disputes in eighteenth- and nineteenth-century Scotland. Now enveloped in clouds of romanticism, much of it stemming from the verses of Stevenson and the novels of Scott, the smaller stones convey the tragedy and the heroism involved in the atrocities of the 1680s without showing the waste, the bigotry and the mutual ignorance. Robert Paterson (1715–1801), the stone mason who spent most of his life after 1758 cutting, re-cutting, and erecting Covenanting stones in Ayrshire, Dumfries-shire and Galloway, is remembered as he was portrayed by Scott as 'Old Mortality', a slightly dotty but not unlovable old man. His crude sculptural work and coarse lettering and epitaphs, often renewed in the nineteenth century, can be seen at Caldons Wood at Glentrool and Auchencloy north of Loch Skerrow, and in the churchyards at Girthon, Anwoth, Kirkcudbright, Kirkandrews, Kells, Balmaghie, Crossmichael, Carsphairn, Dalry, Balmaclellan, Wigtown and Straiton. There are effigies of Paterson by John Currie at Dumfries Museum and in Balmaclellan village, the latter being rather fine work. In addition there are larger monuments, mainly granite obelisks, to be seen in various places—for example, at Kirkconnel (1831), Auchencloy (1835), the Rutherford Monument (1842), above the A75 near Gatehouse, and at Windy Hill in Wigtown (1858).

Churchyards especially worth visiting include:

St Michael's, Dumfries (975757): imposing 1745 church and a huge and fascinating burial area with many fine stones, including one against the south wall of the church to James Ewart of Mulloch, 1839, with shells, cherubs, and grieving figures; and the Burns Mausoleum, 1815, with the marble sculpture by Turnerelli.

Terregles (930770): church with late-sixteenth-century 'Queir' restored in 1875 and with Renaissance monuments inside; outside large plain eighteenth-century stones with superb calligraphy.

Lochrutton (912735): simple 1819 church in impressive situation high above Lochfoot and Lochrutton Loch; good conventional symbolism and section of large sandstone slab with man and woman holding Bible.

Kirkbean (979592): 1776 church with dome-shaped clock tower added 1835; number of classical stones including female figures in eighteenth-century dress, probably ends for tablestones.

Churchyards and memorials

Southwick Old (906569): seventeenth- and eighteenth-century stones, including upright of tablestone in red sandstone with skeleton in high relief with, incised on margin, 'Hodie Mihi Cras Tibi'.

Colvend (862541): 1911 church to plans by P. McGregor Chalmers; several grass-covered late seventeenth- and eighteenth-century stones, including upright with the pious pelican pecking her breast to feed her young, and others with cherubs and floral rosettes.

Urr (816658): fine new church built in 1915; oval churchyard with mausoleum of Herries of Spottes and examples of conventional classical symbolism.

Buittle (808598): 1819 church and ruins of thirteenth-century church; some eighteenth-century stones with poorly executed symbolism; tablestone to Anna Hepburn, 1706, and her spouse, the Rev William Tod, 1713, with Bible and references to three texts; obelisk to David Milligan of Dalskaith, merchant in London, 1798, with fine ship in full sail.

Rerrick Old (760467): seventeenth- and eighteenth-century stones with cherubs and wings, including an upright with an angel blowing a trumpet towards a shield with three goats' heads, and a tablestone to William Graham, 1709, with three scallop shells on a shield.

Kirkcudbright (690511): on the hill above the town and in March a happy place with thousands of crocuses and hundreds of daffodils; the largest collection of uprights and tablestones in Galloway, including three Covenanting stones—'two headless martyrs, hanged and heided cruelly . . .'; a superb tablestone to Samuel Herries, 1793, with six ornate pillars with grotesque figures in East Indian head-dresses, Father Time with his sickle, and a skeleton; several mid-eighteenth-century uprights with the usual cherubs, hour-glasses, and cross-bones, and the trade symbols of the hammermen and the shoemakers, in particular the stones to Alexander Campbell, 1764, Mary McGowan and Samuel Nabany, 1755 and 1776, and John McGouan, 1765; and the Ewart monument (1642) beside the entrance to the yard with interesting versification:

> Our tyme runnes fast as we may sie
> Which being spent then must we die . . .
> I go to grave as to my bed to sleep and ryse again
> I lived in Chryst I died in Chryst I must not heir remane.

Borgue (628483): 1814 church, extended 1899; interesting family group on upright for David McKissock, 1763, with two adult males and a small boy; and the mausoleum to Sir William Gordon of Earlston (1830–1906).

Kirkandrews (600481): excellent site with eighteenth-century stones; upright to James McMonies, 1790, with possible Adam and Eve group.

Balmaghie (722662): small 1794 church on slope above river Dee; one Covenanting stone and mainly plain eighteenth-century stones.

Kells (632783): church built 1822; outstanding collection of early-eighteenth-century stones, with four Garden of Eden sculptures, three of them with Adam and Eve, the tree and the serpent: in particular, the Adam and Eve stones to Agnes Herese and Robert Corson and their children, 1707, and to the children of Roger McNaught and Ann Gordon, 1706; a small upright with a man and a woman holding the scales of justice, John Kennedy, 1732; and the beautiful stone erected by Capt John Gordon in memory of his gamekeeper, John Murray, who died in 1777 after 46 years service, showing his gun, powder-flask, fishing-rod, dog and a gamebird, and on the reverse a suitable and perfectly cut verse by Mr Gillespie, the parish minister (see plate on p 144):

> Ah, John, what changes since I saw thee last;
> Thy fishing and thy shooting days are past.
> Bagpipes and hautboys thou canst sound no more;
> Thy nods, grimaces, winks, and pranks are o'er.
> Thy harmless, queerish, incoherent talk,
> Thy wild vivacity, and trudging walk
> Will soon be quite forget. Thy joys on earth—
> A snuff, a glass, riddles, and noisy mirth—
> Are vanished all. Yet blest, I hope, thou art,
> For, in thy station, weel thou play'dst thy part.

Dalry (618812): church rebuilt 1831; good uprights to James Douglas, 1747, with set square, compass, trowel, and guild cap; Kathleen McCrae, 1762, with cherub and thistle; and James Chapman, 1742; and a tablestone to Thomas Barber, 1771, with floral decoration on the six pillars.

Balmaclellan (651791): church rebuilt c 1835; some small stones with classical and guild symbols.

Girthon Old (605533): seventeenth- and eighteenth-century stones, with especially fine stone to Robert Glover, gardener on the Cally estate, 1775, with his tools, spade, rake, and hoe.

Anwoth Old (583562): wonderfully peaceful site in the old clachan; twelfth-century cross and early-seventeenth-century Renaissance Gordon tomb inside ruined church; Covenanting monuments; excellent eighteenth-century stones with classical symbolism—for example, the upright to John McKioun and Jemigel Heron, 1765:

> Hark from the tomb a doleful sound
> My ears attend the cry
> Ye living men come view the ground
> Where you must shortly lie

and the stone erected by James Carnochan in memory of his children, 1828:

> Stop passengers, as you pass by
> As you are now, so once was I,
> As I am now, so you must be,
> Therefore prepare to follow me.

Kirkmabreck Old (493565): moorland site high above the Cree estuary; some good eighteenth- and nineteenth-century stones, and the granite obelisk with urn to the philosopher Thomas Brown (1777–1820).

Minnigaff (410665): fine small parish church, 1836; medieval crosses in ruined church; eighteenth-century stones include the upright to Margaret Gordon, 1767, and Thomas McCredie, her spouse, smith in Newton Stewart, with his tools, vice, pincers, hammers, files and nails, a Hammermen's Guild cap and mallet, and draperies with tassels in the shape of inverted thistles (see plate on p 144); and another upright to Patrick McClurg in Glenshalloch, 1746, with three ravens pierced with an arrow.

Penninghame Old (411612): heraldic stone in adjacent farmhouse with arms of the Earl of Galloway and a pelican feeding her young; some good eighteenth-century stones including one large figure in the Mochrum style; upright with cherubs and floral and fruit decoration (see plate on p 144):

James Heron in Carnestock who died the 31st October 1758 aged 94 years and Marion Shan his Spouse who died the 10th of March 1748 aged 70 years. Also Mary Jean and Ann Herons their childreen, they left 70 children and Gdr childn Alive and 30 Dead.

Wigtown (435555): with some Covenanting stones and examples of crude seventeenth-century stones; and one sublimely perfect epitaph:

> ... John of honest fame,
> Of stature small and a leg lame;
> Content he was with portion small,
> Keepit shop in Wigtown and that's all.

Kirkcowan (329605): good conventional eighteenth-century stones; for example, the upright to Alexander Dougan, 1716, with skeleton, skull and cross-bones, winged angel, child and coffin.

Sorbie (439468): stones include an upright to George Bean, 1768, with the Hammermen's Guild symbols; and a fragment against the west gable end of the ruined church with rosettes and two trumpet-blowing angels.

Glasserton (421381): interesting mainly eighteenth-century church with later additions; mural monument in north wall of aisle at east end of church to Lady Garlies, c 1590, with rows of male and female heads; good eighteenth-century stones with cherubs and elaborate draperies, including upright to John Conning in Applebie, 1761.

Mochrum (347464): good small village church, 1794; eighteenth-century stones in distinctive local style; for example, upright to John Leyburn in Drumshoge, 1737, with large figure, perhaps a cleric, holding a Bible, with hour-glass, skeleton, coffin, skull, cross-bones, and Father Time (similar examples in Kirkcolm and Penninghame churchyards).

Old Luce (197574): church 1636, rebuilt 1814, outside stairways; classical eighteenth-century stones with floral decorative patterns; for example, upright to William Templeton, 1724.

New Luce (175645): simple small church, 1821; some good eighteenth-century stones, to John McMillan of Lagangarn, 1761, with rosettes and conventional symbolism, and to the McHarg family, 1758, with rosettes, cherubs, Bible, hour-glass, and bluebells.

Inch Old (102608): above the White Loch; excellent conventional symbolism, and interesting stone to Robert McGeoch, 1809, with his tools as a cooper.

Stranraer Old (059608): 1784 church, rebuilt 1841; small area with eighteenth- and nineteenth-century stones with examples of conventional symbolism.

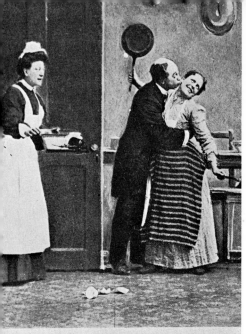

PARODY OF "WHEN THE HEART IS YOUNG."

O, merry go the days
When the heart is young,
When ardent love betrays
That the heart is young;
E'en the bald, the grey, the old,
May be gallant, gay, and bold,
For the maids are seldom cold
When the heart—the heart is young.

Page 143   (*Left*) A local humorous postcard

(*Right*) Sweetheart Abbey, one of several outstanding religious houses in Galloway, a vital link with the medieval heritage now a much-visited tourist attraction

Page 144 (*Above*) The Misses Ruth and Elspeth Macleod pose with the late John Murray, 1777, Kells churchyard; (*below*) the two stones are those of (*left*) James Heron, 1758, Penninghame old churchyard; (*right*) Thomas McCredie, 1737, Minnigaff churchyard

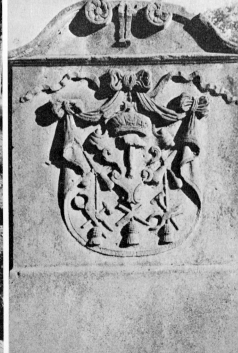

Churchyards and memorials

Kirkcolm Old (030688): eighteenth-century stones include the excellent McMekan group, and a small upright, unique in Galloway, with a four-horse plough team, to 'James McKarzie farmour in Cnockcoyd', 1764.

Portpatrick (NW 999542): for plain stones with data on ship-wrecks and the seventeenth century, or earlier, round tower attached to the ruined church.

Kirkmaiden (124639): magnificent site above Drummore; conventional symbolism and some later stones with representations of ships and a lighthouse; old church c 1633.

References for this chapter are on page 163

APPENDICES

1. Tower houses

Tower houses worth studying (those open to the public are marked AM) include:

Hillis (912726): mid 16c tower by the Maxwells: courtyard with enclosing wall 6½ft high, small 17c gatehouse, and two-storey house built in 1821: restored and occupied.

Drumcoltran (869683) (AM): near Kirkgunzeon: early 16c tower with staircase wing making L plan possibly a late 16c addition: doorway and attic stair turret in re-entrant angle: parapet on single row of corbels.

Buittle Place (818616): north of 13c Balliol courtyard castle; L plan 16c tower into 19c farmhouse; currently under restoration.

Orchardton (816551) (AM): mid 15c tower house by the Cairns family; round exterior but otherwise conventional arrangements; rectangular rooms include first floor hall cum private chapel with aumbry with piscina; wheel-stair to cape-house and parapet walk.

Threave (739622) (AM): late 14c castle of the Douglas Lords of Galloway; outer enclosure area; 1513 courtyard wall 5ft thick with drum towers at the corners and keyhole and dumbbell gunports; massive five-storey tower, 70ft high, walls 8ft thick, main vault 25ft high; access by boat across river Dee (see plate on p 35).

Barscobe (659806): L plan laird's house, 1648, by Wm MacLellan; two storeys and attic; note absence of parapet at wallhead level; pleasant attic dormer windows; restored 1972.

Earlston (612840): L plan laird's house, 1655, by Wm Gordon; wheel-stair corbelled out over re-entrant angle.

MacLellans Castle (682511) (AM): large town house by Sir Thomas MacLellan of Bombie, 1582; essentially domestic architecture on variation of L plan plus south-east tower; arms in panels above doorway in re-entrant angle; gunports; corner turrets.

Appendix 1

Barmagachan (613494): laird's house, 1698, by Ephraim Mac-Lellan; rectangular block with two wings; steep pitched roof; to west of motte.

Plunton (604507): on site of 13c moated manor; 16c L plan tower house by McGhies or Lennoxes; corner turrets with ornamental corbelling; in ruins.

Rusco (584604): late 15c or early 16c tower by Carsons or Gordons; 17c annexe to north; parapet walk and cape-house with chequer-wise corbelling; upper structure wrecked in World War II by Glasgow evacuees.

Cardoness (591553) (AM): mid 15c rectangular tower on very strong site by the McCullochs; four storeys and attic; parapet walk flush with walling; 53ft high walls 8ft thick; keyhole gun-ports; splendid hall and solar fireplaces, stone window seats and aumbries.

Barholm (520529): L plan late 16c or early 17c tower by McCul-lochs; doorway in re-entrant angle with rich cabled hood-moulding with two masks and grotesque animals; charming tiny window details.

Carsluith (494541) (AM): late 15c or early 16c rectangular tower of the Browns with north wing added 1568 to form L plan; east and west parapet walks, corner turrets with cannon gargoyles.

Garlies (422691): late 15c or early 16c tower by the Stewarts, later summer residence of the Earls of Galloway; fireplace with rich but damaged moulding including hunting scene; inner yard 48ft by 53ft, and outer enclosure 140ft by 125ft.

Castle Stewart (379690): later 16c or 17c tower in ruins; good third-floor fireplace with moulded cornice; foundations of subsidiary buildings to east.

Baldoon (425536): later 17c gateway with two piers with lozenge and diamonded decoration; fragment of the Dunbars' tower nearby.

Place of Sorbie (451470): marsh site near 12c motte; large L plan tower c 1585 by the Hannays; spacious main stairway to first-floor hall; stairway to upper floors corbelled out over entrance with corbel termination in human head; corner turrets.

The Isle (476365): at north end of Isle of Whithorn; L plan tower, 1674, by Patrick Huston; reconstructed in 19c and restored in last ten years.

Place of Dowies (381430): late 16c Maxwell L plan tower; altered as farmhouse in 19c; courtyard range of buildings; in ruins.

Myrton (360432): early 16c rectangular McCulloch tower built in motte, with 17c adjacent additions; in ruins.

Place of Mochrum (308541): two tower houses within courtyard area, both built by the Dunbars, the west tower c 1500, rectangular, with parapet walk and angle turrets, and the east tower c 1580 with separate projecting staircase wing on north side; restored 1876 and later.

Carscreugh (223598): central block with two square flanking towers c 1680; in ruins.

Park (188571) (AM): plain well-preserved L plan laird's house by Thomas Hay in 1590; steep roof with crow-stepped gables; massive chimney stacks, third-floor attic stair turret.

Castle Kennedy (111609): originally island site; central block with two flanking towers each with high smaller towers in re-entrant angles; by Earl of Cassilis in 1607 on site of earlier tower; destroyed by fire 1716.

Craigcaffie (088641): well-preserved rectangular tower by John Neilson c 1575 on swamp site; small building with grandiose pretensions, wall walks, machicolation above doorway, and gargoyles.

Chappell or Castle of St John (061608): L plan Adair town house c 1520, heightened in 17c; important as a fascinating example of a town gaol, post 1815, with cells and iron gates with chains in upper two floors.

Corsewall (NW 991714): 15c rectangular tower on slight mound in swamp area; fragmentary remains.

Lochnaw (NW 991628): 16c Agnew tower house replacing castle on island site in loch; 1663 and 1704 and later buildings round courtyard.

Dunskey (003533): Immensely spectacular Iron Age and medieval promontory site; probably mid 16c Adair L plan tower house with west range, at the south side of a 40ft wide ditch; ruinous and dangerous.

2. Source documents on the rising of the Levellers

(a) *An Account of the Reasons of Some People in Galloway, their Meetings anent Public Grievances through Inclosures* (extract)

To complete our ruin they have now proceeded beyond all the bounds of former years from the sense of the greatness of their gain to add to their former enclosures. They this year have warned a very great number of families to remove at Whitsunday, the 15th of May, 1724, viz: upwards of sixty in some parishes and more than thirty in others, and scarce any other places can be found out for their relief, so that we expected nothing but the open fields for ourselves, wives and little ones, and our substance to be dispersed and wasted; and thus almost distracted by hearing the doleful cries and lamentations of our wives and children we did arise in a considerable body, without any arms or ammunition, until we were necessitate for self-preservation in respect of a Order publicly intimated at the Kirk doors upon a Lord's Day that all heritors, life-renters, wadsetters and free holders were to appear with their best horses, arms, and ammunition to make an engagement upon us; but they seeing our numbers very far to exceed theirs, did not adventure and ever since we have kept some small quantity of arms for our own defence lest at any time we should be surprised by them; but our far greater number have nothing but staves or clubs to drive the Irish cattle, of which we have seized upon and slaughtered fifty-three, and liekas secured twelve barrels of run brandy which we delivered to the King's Officers and is now in the Custom House at Kirkcudbright. We have thrown down some of these de-populating inclosures which have been made contrary to all the precepts and commands contained in the Word of God. . . .

We would be willing to take the lands which were parked as they were set formerly, and further to pay the interest of the money laid out in enclosing ground; likeas from the example of our superiors, our very equals have undertaken to add fuel unto our oppression, for some country tenants, or rather drovers, have taken all the grounds they can get and stockt the same with black cattle and sheep by which many an honest man is straitened as well as by the gentlemen's parks themselves. . . . And lately the said Mr Basil Hamilton hath cast out thirteen families upon the 22nd day of May instant who are lying by the dykesides. Neither will he suffer them to erect any shelter or covering at the dykesides to preserve their little ones from the injury of the cold, which cruelty is very like the accomplishment of that threatening of the Jacobites at the late rebellion, that they would make Galloway a hunting field, because of our public appearance for his Majesty King George at Drumfries, and our opposition against them at that time in their wicked designs.

(b) *Letter of James Clerk, Kirkcudbright to Sir John Clerk, Edinburgh 3 June 1724* (extract)

On Sunday the 31st the mob gave generall orders at twelve Parish Church doors, for all men and women to assemble together with their best arms as formerly, on Tuesday the 2nd currt, at the Boat of Rouan, a ferry upon the Dee on the confines of a large and beautiful forrest, about ten miles from this town.

The troops having courriers had timeous notice of them put themselves in order to receive them, and on Tuesday about three in the morning Major Ducarey, the Commander, set out from hence with two troops of Horse and four troops on foot. He placed one troop of horse in front which he himself headed. The four troops on foot commanded by Lord Crighton and Capt Auchinleck made up the main body, and the other troop of Horse commanded by Capt Nugene brought up the rear. We arrived at the place appointed about eight in the morning, and finding to our dissapointment no appearance, halted three hours, in which time the men refreshed themselves and the Horse were turned to grass. About twelve there crossed the river and came up to us severall country gentlemen who, as well as we, were surprized that the Levellers had made no appearance that day, upon which orders were given to march back to the town again. When in our march backwards we had arrived at the Steps of Tarf, a message comes to the major informing that the countrey gentlemen had fallen upon a small party of them of about 50 in number, and had taken sundry prisoners, but in danger of having them rescued without assistance of the forces. Upon which the Major detaches 30 horse to advance with speed to their relief to the place which was on a hill about a mile from us, ordering the men to halt till account of the matter was sent to him.

This party of a mob of about 50 were all armed with guns, pitchforks and poles. Upon the gentlemens advancing to them, they kept them off with their pitchforks and clubs. One of them pushed at Mr Basil Hamilton with a pitchfork which happened to flance athwart his breast, otherwise if right directed would have prov'd mortall. Another of them struck Mr Heron twice with a hanger but was as many times putt off. Another gentleman was almost knockt off his horse, the women all the while plying them with stones, so that they had work enough among their hands, and would have come off but indifferently had not the detachment of the Horse immediately come up to their assistance. As soon as the mobb saw them they made off but the horsemen rode up among them sword in hand, disarmed and took 14 of them prisoners, one of which had his ear sliced off to a stitch, besides a large cut in the neck. All being dispersed they brought off the prisoners, came up with us, and joyn'd our main body, upon which they were ordered into the same posture as before and marched directly into town where we arrived at eight at night, a sufficient guard having conveyed the prisoners to the town house.

3. Planned villages and country houses

(a) Estate and Planned Villages

Village	Date	Founder(s)
CASTLE DOUGLAS	1791	William Douglas
CREETOWN	1791	James McCulloch
DALBEATTIE	c 1781	Alexander Copland and George Maxwell
GARLIESTON	c 1790	Lord Garlies
GATEHOUSE-OF-FLEET	post 1775	James Murray
KIRKANDREWS*	c 1795	—
KIRKCOWAN	post 1793	John and Robert Milroy
KIRKPATRICK-DURHAM	c 1785	Rev Dr David Lamont
NEWTON DOUGLAS	1789	William Douglas
PORT LOGAN	1818	Col Andrew McDowall
PORT WILLIAM	c 1776	Sir William Maxwell
SOUTHERNESS	c 1790	Richard Oswald
TONGLAND†	1790	James Murray
TWYNHOLM	c 1795	Lord Daer

* Reported in *Statistical Account* and other sources, but never built
† See description below; never started

(b) Village to be Built at Tongueland

Mr Murray of Broughton having determined to have a Village upon the Clauchan of Tongueland, he has got a regular plan for the same, by which there is to be a square in the middle, and three principal streets; and most excellent water will be brought into a square for the benefit of the inhabitants, from a very fine spring in the neighbourhood.

The situation of the Village will command a most delightful view of the river, the town of Kirkcudbright, St Mary's Isle, and the Rosses.

It is little more than a mile from Kirkcudbright; the tide flows up the river, so that large ships can come up and discharge at the

Village, where there is a safe well sheltered harbour; and upon the banks of the river are most convenient situations for warehouses, stores, etc. and there is no doubt trade may be carried on to great advantage as the Village will be free of those dues and burdens, payable by the inhabitants to the burgh of Kirkcudbright. Mr Murray will be willing to grant feu rights, on reasonable terms, for houses and yeards, to those who chuse to build; and he intends to inclose and subdivide the farm of Clauchan of Tongueland, so as to have it in his power to accommodate the inhabitants with suitable fields.

For further particulars apply to Mr Bushby at Tinwalddouns; Mr Buchanan at Kirkcudbright; or John Thompson at Boreland, the factor.

(*Dumfries Weekly Journal*, 2 February 1790)

(c) *Letter from Robert Mylne to Lord Garlies about the New House to be built at Cally for James Murray of Broughton. Rome 25 January 1759*

I have sent a sketch for Mr Murray's house, which I am hopeful he will be so good as to think, as the bad digested principalls that a house should be built upon, rather than a house that I say is fit for him . . . The situation is supposed to be on a small rising ground . . . an extended plan before, for prospect: and the hill rising behind to preserve it from cold winds. This house is divided into 4 stories. The first is for the use of all servants who work in the house. It holds the kitchen and all the nauseous places that should not be seen or smelt by company. It is half sunk in the ground to keep it cooll, and half above to give it light, and make a pedestall to the whole building. The entrance to it is by the private stair at one end to keep the front free of the drudgery servants . . . The second storey is entirely apropriated fro the reception and entertainment of strangers . . . the third storey is all the bed-chambers for the master, company and children of the house. The fourth storey is rooms for the principall servants, nursery, and a few rooms for more company. The garrets are for the lower servants who work in the house . . .

In the ground storey, A is a hall which gives admittance to all the rooms on this levell without going through one another. It is lighted from the stair and must be painted very white. B is the larder, which as it should be cooll, is turned to the north. C is the servants hall, placed in this corner that their noise may be out of hearing . . . I is the stewards counting room, it lyes next the private stair and entry, and has a door from thence for to admit those people who have business with him . . . L is the kitchen, which as it should be clean and cooll, is turned to the morning sun and coolness of the north. It is placed under the library to keep its disagreeable smell from the rooms where company are. M is the coall house, by the windows of which, the coalls may be thrown in from the carts . . .

For the principall storey, A is the great hall from which there is admittance to every room without going through one another. In the middle of it are 2 square pillars to support a wall in the 3rd storey. B is the small dining parlour . . . C is the drawing room and is placed here for the company to retire to . . . D is the grand dining room . . . E is the great stair, open from top to bottom . . . If the quality of the rooms are not according to Mr Murray's way of life it is easily altered. If the measures of the whole house are too large or too small, decrease or enlarge the scale . . .

4. Source documents from the Broughton and Cally Muniments

(a) *Tack of a Tenement at Gatehouse, 25 October 1763*

It is agreed and Ended by James Murray . . . and William Johnston shoemaker in Kirkcudbright . . . that . . . James Murray . . . Doth hereby Bind and oblige himself . . . to Build or cause be Built and have in readiness against the term of Whitsunday next a house of the Demensions following . . . Thirty feet in front of length and Eighteen in widness over the walls and Eleven feet high in the side walls . . . upon the Ground on the south side of the new Great Road leading from the Gatehouse to the Bridge of Fleet The front of the said house to be fifteen feet distant from the said road and at each end of the said house to Erect a Shade Eighteen feet wide over the walls and 12' 6" long and 7' 6" high leaving a space of 30" at each end for a passage to the Garden . . . a piece of Ground . . . 137' from the Back wall in length and 60' in Breadth . . . in Tack . . . for the space of 38 years . . .

The said James Murray being hereby bound to provide the said William Johnston with Grass for one Cow in Summer betwixt the old road which did lead from the Gatehouse to the foord in the Fleet during the first three years of this lease . . .

. . . William Johnston . . . obliges himself . . . sufficiently to pave and Causeway 15' forward from the front of his house to the said Great Road . . . and . . . obliges himself . . . that he . . . shall not . . . Directly or indirectly sell in retail any wine ale or Spirituous Liquors of any kind nor keep a Publick house or house of Entertainment without special licence or liberty in writing from . . . James Murray . . . Nor shall he . . . Smuggle or be directly or indirectly concerned in Smuggling or importing from the Isle of Man any Counterhand or Smuggled Goods or Merchandise whatsoever . . .

Appendix 4

(b) *Tack of Parks in Tormick, 12 May, 1777*

Matthew Buchanan factor for James Murray . . . hereby setts the parks of land . . . in that part of Filillarg called Tormick . . . the number of the Parks being reckoned from the Stone dike on the North march of the farm of Gatehouse . . . Park No 1st at 14 Shillings pr. Acre to Robert Richardson Shoemaker at Gatehouse and James McClellan labourer . . . Park No 2d at 12 Shillings Ster. pr. acre to Andrew Carter weaver at Gatehouse and John McTaggart taylor . . . Park No 3d at 15 Shillings and sixpence Ster. pr. acre to James Porter Shoemaker at Gatehouse . . . Park No 4th . . . to David McTaggart taylor at Gatehouse . . . Park No 5th . . . to Patrick Hughan . . .

All the acres to be . . . by the measurement of Wm Dunbar in Townhead or any other land Surveyor employed . . .

The tenants within the tack to lay over the land with lime not under fifty Carlisle bushels to each acre or with Shells not under twenty Tons each acre: one half to each park to be in pasturage only the last four years of the Let, and the other half to be well dunged the last year . . The Master is to complete the fencing against the end of this month . . . and to give bars for the Gateway into each park . . .

(c) *Memorandum left by Mr Murray with John Bushby, 23 January 1775, dealing with the management of his estates in his absence*

Broughton . . . The Large Marle bog is already open and the drain completely finished but there are other bogs in which it is supposed there are considerable quantitys of Marle contained, and if Drains can be made at a moderate expense it might be proper to open them . . .

Plunton . . . This Farm is presently sett for £90 Sterg. per year— Mr Murray offered it to the Tenants for £200 a year, and they offered £160 Sterg. a year—It contains 460 Acres and is a valuable Farm, but has been under very bad management and therefore on Mr Murrays setting his Shire Lands, he intended to have it taken into his own hands and to have keept it as a Stock Farm for a few years, until he got it into some heart, but as this plan cannot immediately be carried into execution he would agree to continue the present Tenants for two years . . .

Culnaughtry, contains upwards of 600 acres, but its quite in the state of nature, it pays at present £60 a year and Mr Murray thinks a hundred has been offered for it, but he considers it to be of advantage to him as it would save a great expence in dykes to let this Farm and the Farm of Auchenleck together . . . which contains about 200 acres and is now sett at £12 yearly and the two Farms together Mr Murray thinks they should sett at £130 Sterg. a year on a 19 Years Lease—These Farms will not do to manage them as they have hitherto been managed but are very favourably situated for Lime and to encourage the Tenants to use Lime which it is their own Interest to do, Mr. Murray would furnish at the nearest landing place 1000 Bushels of Shell Lime for Kirkcassal and 600 Bushells for Culnaughtry and Auchenleck . . .

Drumruck Murraytoun and Orquhers . . . The present Rent is about £140 yearly but Mr Murray expects a very great rise upon these farms . . . he imagines they will bring more than Double the present Rent, he has been informed the tenant keep 3000 Sheep between 30 and 40 Milk Cows and sells yearly about a hundred Stotts which he keeps over Summer and perhaps part of them over Winter and he also has 800 goats—He has also sufficient Corn Land for two families . . .

5. Members of the House of Commons, 1741–90

Wigtownshire
James Stewart	1741–7
John Stewart	47–54
James Stewart	54–61
John Hamilton	61–2
James Murray	62–8
Keith Stewart	68–84
Andrew McDouall	84–90

Wigtown Burghs
William Stewart	1741–7
James Stewart	47–54
John Hamilton	54–61
Archibald Montgomerie	61–2
Keith Stewart	62
John Hamilton	62–8
George Augustus Selwyn	68
Chauncy Townsend	68–70
William Stewart	70–4
William Norton	74–5
Henry Watkin Dashwood	75–80
William Adam	80–4
William Dalrymple	84–90

Stewartry of Kirkcudbright
Basil Hamilton	1741–2
John Maxwell	42–7
John (Ross) Mackye	47–68
James Murray	68–74
William Stewart	74–80
Peter Johnston	80–1
John Gordon	81–2
Peter Johnston	82–6
Alexander Stewart	86–90

Dumfries Burghs
Lord John Johnstone	1741–3
Sir James Johnstone	43–54
Archibald Douglas	54–61
Thomas Miller	61–6
James Montgomery	66–8
William Douglas	68–80
Sir Robert Herries	80–84
Sir James Johnstone	84–90

References and Bibliography

Good general bibliographies of Dumfries and Galloway are provided in the *Third Statistical Account of Scotland* vol XIV, *The Counties of Kirkcudbright and Wigtown* (Glasgow 1965), and vol XII, *The County of Dumfries* (Glasgow 1962), while Ian Donnachie's *Industrial Archaeology of Galloway* (Newton Abbot 1971) has a detailed bibliography of primary and secondary sources on regional social and economic history.

Abbreviations used

GV	General View of the Agriculture of . . .
IA	Industrial Archaeology
NLS	National Library of Scotland, Edinburgh
NSA	New (Second) Statistical Account
OS	Ordnance Survey
OSA	Old (First) Statistical Account
PRO	Public Record Office, London
RCAHMS	Royal Commission on the Ancient and Historical Monuments of Scotland
SGM	Scottish Geographical Magazine
SHR	Scottish Historical Review
SL	Signet Library, Edinburgh
SP	Session Papers of the Court of Session
SRO	Scottish Record Office, Register House, Edinburgh
SRS	Scottish Record Society Publication
TDGNHAS	Transactions of the Dumfries and Galloway Natural History and Antiquarian Society

Chapter One. History and heritage
The best regional history is still Sir H. Maxwell's *A History of Dumfries and Galloway* (Edinburgh 1896), although this is almost wholly concerned with pre-eighteenth-century developments. The two Statistical Account volumes mentioned above are probably the most useful modern accounts, while J. F. Robertson's *The Story of Galloway* (Castle Douglas 1963) makes popular reading.

References and Bibliography

Chapter Two. Andrew Symson's Galloway
The extracts from Symson's *Description* are from Maitland's 1823 ed. For an old but reliable essay see W. J. Couper, 'Andrew Symson: Preacher, Printer and Poet', *SHR* 13 (1915–16). Household returns for the Machars parishes are included in the *Parish Lists of Wigtownshire and Minnigaff*, *SRS* (1916). For the Pont maps see J. C. Stone, 'An Evaluation of the Nidisdaile Manuscript Map by Timothy Pont' and D. G. Moir and R. A. Skelton, 'New Light on the First Atlas of Scotland', both in *SGM* 84 (1968).

Chapter Three. Tower houses
For general social and economic conditions the vols published privately by the 4th Marquis of Bute are invaluable, especially *Kirkcudbright Town Council Records 1576–1604* (1939) and a similar vol for 1606–58 (1958). These can be consulted in the Ewart Library, Dumfries, as can typescripts by R. C. Reid of Glover's and Gairdner's protocol books. P. Hume Brown's *Early Travellers in Scotland* (1891) and D. Defoe's *Tour through Britain* (1724–6) have useful Galloway references. For Scottish tower house architecture see S. Cruden, *The Scottish Castle* (1963) and for Galloway lists see W. Mackenzie's *History of Galloway* (1841) and the RCAHMS vols for *Wigtown* (1912) and *Kirkcudbright* (1914).

Chapter Four. Witches and Covenanters
For a thorough analysis of different strands of seventeenth-century life and thought see C. Hill, *Anti-Christ in Seventeenth Century England* (1971), K. Thomas, *Religion and the Decline in Magic* (1971) and A. Macfarlane, *Witchcraft in Tudor and Stuart England* (1970). A detailed list of Scottish witchcraft cases is contained in G. F. Black, *A Calander of Cases of Witchcraft in Scotland 1510–1727* (1938). Published record material includes the *Register of the Synod of Galloway 1664–71* (1856) and two further vols *The Session Book of Penninghame 1696–1724* (1933) and *The Session Book of Minnigaff 1694–1750* (1939). For an assessment of the vast literature on the Covenanters see I. B. Cowan, 'The Covenanters: A Revision Article', *SHR* 47 (1968).

Chapter Five. The Agrarian Revolution and the Levellers
For general social and economic background see H. Hamilton, *An Economic History of Scotland in the Eighteenth Century* (1963) and T. C. Smout, *A History of the Scottish People 1560–1830* (1969). Agrarian change is described in J. E. Handley's, *Scottish Farming in the Eighteenth Century* (1953). Developments in south-west Scotland are described in J. Webster, *GV of the Agriculture of Galloway* (1794) and S. Smith's vol

with the same title (1810), while Sir John Sinclair's *Statistical Account* contains a wealth of local data relating to agriculture and social conditions. Two useful articles are A. S. Morton, 'The Levellers of Galloway', *TDGNHAS* 19 (1933–5) and W. A. J. Prevost, 'Letters Reporting the Rising of the Levellers in 1724', *TDGNHAS* 44 (1967), both drawing heavily on key documents in the SRO and NLS. *The Caledonian Mercury* reports the course of the Rising, and a number of contemporary pamphlets on enclosure and the Levellers can be consulted in the NLS.

Chapter Six. The landscape of improvement
Robert Heron's descriptions of Gatehouse, Newton Douglas, Castle Douglas and Kirkpatrick-Durham are all valuable, as are most of the relevant parish entries in the *OSA* and in Chalmer's *Caledonia* vol 5. The material on which the account of Gatehouse is based comes from SRO GD 10, the Broughton and Cally Muniments. John Butt's 'Industrial Archaeology of Gatehouse-of-Fleet', *IA* 3 (1966) and I. Macleod's *Gatehouse-of-Fleet and Ferrytown of Cree* (1969) provide descriptions of surviving remains. There is much useful material on Lamont and Kirkpatrick-Durham in W. A. Stark's *Book of Kirkpatrick-Durham* (1903). A useful collection of essays on the British country house is H. Colvin and J. Harris (eds) *The Country Seat: Studies in the History of the British Country House* (1970). For estate maps see I. Adams, *The Mapping of a Scottish Estate* (1971) and the Roy maps are dealt with in R. A. Skelton, 'The Military Survey of Scotland 1747–55', *SGM* 83 (1967). A fine collection of prints with useful text is W. Daniell and R. Ayton's *A Picturesque Voyage Round the Coast of Gt. Britain* (1814–22), available in university libraries or the NLS.

Chapter Seven. Robert Heron's Galloway
The fundamental source is Robert Heron's *Observations Made in a Journey thr' the Western Counties of Scotland in the Autumn of 1792* (Perth and Edinburgh 1793, 2nd ed 1799), which provides a great deal of valuable contemporary material for most of Dumfries and Galloway. Heron can be supplemented by the *OSA*'s and *GV*'s *of Agriculture*, described in the references for Chapter Five.

Chapter Eight. Landowners and industry
The account of Sir William Douglas is based on research for Ian Donnachie's *IA of Galloway*, supplemented by material in the SRO, especially the Melville Castle Muniments GD 51/1/32, letters between Henry Dundas and James Shaw, and the Abercromby of Forglen Muniments GD 185/40, Submission and History of the House of

References and Bibliography

Douglas and Shaw, Abstract of the Will of Sir Wm Douglas 1790, Remarks by Samuel Douglas 1823. Douglas's landed and banking interests are covered in several Signet Library series, including SP 556/43 Petition of Wm Young, Cashier of the Galloway Bank 1820, and SP 379/18 Wm Douglas of Castle Douglas v John Maxwell 1797. The *OSA* has much on his agricultural, industrial and community schemes, while extensive transport interests are evidenced in SL SP 262/9 Shawes v Douglas and others 1811. There is a chapter on Douglas in A. Trotter's *East Galloway Sketches* (1901). A full list of records relating to James Murray's estates can be inspected in the SRO in GD 10 Broughton and Cally Muniments. For his association with banking see the *Report of the Committee on Douglas, Heron & Co, Bankers in Air* (1776-8). For land development and changes see the *OSA* and *GV's of Agriculture*.

Chapter Nine. Politics and society in eighteenth-century Galloway
Useful material on economic and social background is provided by two publications of the 4th Marquis of Bute: *The Session Book of Penninghame 1724-49* (1933) and *The Session Book of Wigtown 1701-45* (1934). Biographical sketches of Galloway gentlemen and a political survey of Scottish constituencies are included in L. B. Namier and J. Brooke, *The House of Commons 1754-90* (1964) and R. Sedgwick, *The House of Commons 1715-54* (1970). Letters by and relating to the 7th Earl of Galloway are included in A. Aspinall, *The Later Correspondence of George III*, vol 1, 1783-93 (1962) and vol 4, 1802-7 (1968).

Chapter Ten. Life and labour, 1800-1900
The most valuable source for the period to 1845 is the second *Statistical Account* (NSA), vol 4 covering Dumfries and Galloway. The parish entries vary in quality, but most contain useful descriptive and quantitative data. Numerous parish and local histories are available, among the best being D. Frew's *The Parish of Urr* (1909) and G. Fraser's *Wigtown and Whithorn* (1877). Parliamentary papers of the period contain an immense quantity of information on agriculture, industry and social conditions. A full list is given in the *IA of Galloway*, and census data is available after 1801. The first OS map series became available after 1850. Many parish records are still held locally. The standard work on family history is P. H. M'Kerlie's *History of the Lands and their Owners in Galloway* (1877). Many articles and papers on nineteenth-century life can readily be consulted in the *TDGNHAS*.

Chapter Eleven. Ports and harbours of Solway shore
For a full account of trade and shipping in the Solway ports after 1700

References and Bibliography

see I. Donnachie's *IA of Galloway*, ch 5. There is extensive documentation on this topic in estate and Customs & Excise papers, mainly at the SRO and PRO, London. Maps and plans can usefully be consulted in either the SRO or NLS Map Room. Ports and harbours in Galloway are covered in PP 1847 XXXII *Report of the Commissioners on Tidal Harbours,* and on the W ports in particular, PP 1809 III *Report from the Select Committee on Telford's Report and Survey relative to Communication between England and Ireland.* I. Macleod has edited a useful account of *Shipping in Dumfries and Galloway in 1820* (1972), and there is much interesting material on local shipping in the libraries at Stranraer, Kirkcudbright and Dumfries.

Chapter Twelve. Victorian and Edwardian tourists
An important source for the history of tourism during the period are the many guide books cited in the chapter. A number of more local guides were also published and contain a wealth of social history. There is no shortage of material on the history of railways, and D. Smith's *Little Railways of South-West Scotland* (1969) and C. Highet's *The Glasgow and South-Western Railway* (1965) are useful introductions. The history of tourism in Britain remains to be written, and thus the local research potential is considerable.

Chapter Thirteen. Churchyards and memorials
For Scottish churches see G. Hay *The Architecture of Scottish Post-Reformation Churches 1560–1843* (1957) and I. G. Lindsay *The Scottish Parish Kirk* (1960).

Acknowledgements

This book owes much to the assistance and advice of the staff of numerous national, university and local libraries, including; Glasgow University Library; The Mitchell Library, Glasgow; Andersonian Library, University of Strathclyde; Aberdeen University Library; the National Library of Scotland; the Scottish Record Office; Public Record Office; Signet Library, Edinburgh; Ewart Library, Dumfries; Kirkcudbright County Library; Wigtownshire County Library; the Stewartry Museum; and Dumfries Burgh Museum.

It would be difficult to acknowledge the help of so many individuals, but we owe special thanks to the following: Dr J. K. St Joseph, University of Cambridge; A. E. Truckell, Dumfries Burgh Museum; the Earl and Countess of Galloway; Mrs E. Murray Usher; Dr John Butt and John Hume of the University of Strathclyde.

For help in photographic research and for permission to reproduce photographs we are grateful to the libraries of Aberdeen, Glasgow and Edinburgh Universities; George Edwards; Dr H. C. Lang; Dr J. K. St Joseph; Studio Maxwell, Castle Douglas; the National Monuments Record of Scotland; and T. C. B. Phin of the *Dumfries and Galloway Standard*.

The maps were drawn by Miss Morag Warwick and the typescript was prepared at various stages by Miss Patricia Slater, Miss Pauline Lisney and Miss Betty Wilson.

Our task of research and writing would certainly have been more difficult and less enjoyable had we been denied the helpful consideration of all these and many other people.

I.D. and I.M.

Kirkcudbright

Index

The index is divided into two sections: PLACES AND PERSONS and SUBJECTS. References to illustrations are indicated in italics

Index

Index

Index